Estranged

Leaving Family and Finding Home

A MEMOIR

Jessica Berger Gross

SCRIBNER

New York London Toronto Sydney New Delhi

SCRIBNER

An Imprint of Simon & Schuster, Inc.

1230 Avenue of the Americas

New York, NY 10020

First Scribner hardcover edition July 2017

SCRIBNER and design are registered trademarks of The Gale Group, Inc., used under license by Simon & Schuster, Inc., the publisher of this work.

For information about special discounts for bulk purchases, please contact Simon & Schuster Special Sales at 1-866-506-1949 or business@simonandschuster.com.

The Simon & Schuster Speakers Bureau can bring authors to your live event. For more information or to book an event, contact the Simon & Schuster Speakers Bureau at 1-866-248-3049 or visit our website at www.simonspeakers.com.

Interior design by Kyle Kabel

Manufactured in the United States of America

1   3   5   7   9   10   8   6   4   2

ISBN 978-1-5011-0160-1
ISBN 978-1-5011-0162-5 (ebook)

Portions of Chapter 12 originally appeared in a December 20, 2013, *New York Times Magazine* essay entitled "Life with Bella."

For Neil
And for Lucien

Estranged

ONE

MY FATHER SAID I was the one who started things. That what happened, that what he did to me, was *my* fault. He and my mother said I was fresh, a back-talker. I was too loud, too opinionated, and too smart for my own good. I was too messy. My brothers nicknamed me Messy Jessie. I *was* messy, just like I was argumentative and full of opinions. So some days I tried to go against my nature. I tried to be quiet. I tried to be a good girl. If only I could say or do the exact right thing, if only I could make myself ever so slightly disappear.

But I couldn't control my father's moods, and I never knew when a good day would take a dangerous turn. The best I could do was look for clues to his emotional state, warning signs that signaled trouble. I learned to fear his white V-neck undershirt and oldest paint-splattered jeans, the open can of Budweiser, the smells of turpentine and grease as he worked around the house or under one of the family cars, and the heavy-duty cream he kept by the sink to get the dirt off his hands and out from under his fingernails. Bills spread on the kitchen table. Frustrations at work. An argument with my mother. And on the worst days, the salt and pepper shakers or shoe or phone thrown at me from across the room, the fists and terrible words. I was a selfish bitch. I was spoiled rotten. I was asking for it.

My first memory. I must have been three or four. I remember my father chasing after me. His flat palm made contact with my small pale back. I can still picture myself running from him, pulling up my nightgown, and turning my head over one shoulder, straining to see myself in the hallway mirror. A moment later he was gone, fled down the stairs, but the pink mark of his hand remained.

My parents believed in corporal punishment. My father rolled up a newspaper to threaten the dog for peeing inside the house, and sometimes followed through with a whack. When I was very young, I was given the occasional spanking. My father would sit on a kitchen chair and put me over his lap, pulling down my ruffled underwear to reveal the peach moons of my buttocks. And then came the measured number of hand slaps to what my mother, who was watching, called my tushie.

This was different. When my father turned mean, he lost control. His face changed color. Red angry screams. I ran and hid in my mother's closet. I curled up into a ball. I peered out through the rows of my mother's silky dresses and scratchy slacks, checking to see whether it was safe to come out.

I hated having him mad at me. I hated being bad. I remember one of those days when, as a sort of psychology experiment, I decided to do everything, be everything, he could possibly want; to be perfect. I'd finish all the chores he asked me to do and then some. I'd bring him salted peanuts and shut up already on the couch. I pretended we were in the army and he was my drill sergeant and I was a new recruit in basic training. I practically called him *sir*.

He exploded anyway. I knew what was coming.

His rage was a runaway train. I had to decide whether to let him have me right away, or try to escape and chance angering him further. I decided to risk it and run. But he chased me to the stairs and trapped me so that my back was against the stairwell wall. My breath caught. I covered my face with my arms.

Please don't hurt me.

There was nobody I could ask for help. So I asked him, the most powerful person I knew.

Please, no, I said. *Please. No!*

He raised his right arm. I didn't know how hard the impact would be or how much it would hurt this time. But I knew his hands. They were dry and rough and meaty. I was afraid I would break and shatter when he put them on me.

I braced for what came next. My body hardened, my muscles tensed and tightened, even as my mind shut down.

Time suspended.

Then it was over. He was spent, and there'd be no more yelling or hitting. Afterward it was still and quiet. Like a heavy blanket of snow falling in the predawn while the neighborhood sleeps. Because afterward, when he was ashamed, he would never bother me.

Occasionally I went and found my mother propped up on pillows in their bedroom, grading a stack of papers. She wore a satiny bathrobe and had tortoiseshell combs pushing back the feathery wings of her brown hair, and slept under a sunflower-gold comforter. There was no need to explain. She couldn't change him, but scratching my back with her long oval nails, she'd read to me. Other times she was nowhere to be found. And so I'd take refuge in my room. I'd shut the door and wrap my arms around my body, hugging my knees to my chest and comforting myself in bed with my books and stuffed animals.

My father's words hurt even worse than the hitting, because words lasted long after the marks faded. They lasted forever.

Bitch. Which meant I was a bad girl, the worst girl. *JAP*. Which meant I was a spoiled brat. *Cunt*. I didn't know what that one meant, only that it was the C-word and had to do with my vagina and made me feel dirty. I was a *stupid piece of shit,* he told me. I was rude, inconsiderate, selfish, self-centered. I was a liar.

On those very worst days, my mother had her share of cruel words for me, too. I was a naughty girl. I always thought I was right. I never listened. She said I'd been *cruising for a bruising*. She said I was too much trouble. More trouble than I was worth. *Good for nothing*. My mother didn't hit me, but she didn't know how to protect me, either. Instead, she warned me. *You have it coming.*

Or she wouldn't say anything, and that was supposed to be sympathy, but it was nothing close to enough.

* * *

The summer before I started second grade, my mother landed a job as a reading teacher in a school district on the south shore of Long Island. We went shopping for a new house so she wouldn't have to commute.

"Every few years we move," my mother said, sighing, on the way to meet the real estate agent.

We'd left Centerport, in Long Island's Suffolk County, and the house where I'd lived as a baby, after swastikas were spray-painted on our mailbox. In Plainview, a suburban town in Nassau County, twenty minutes closer to New York City, and with plenty of Jewish families, I had a big room with yellow wallpaper and a window facing the street.

"This will be our fourth time," my father added. He smiled. Like the Jeffersons, we were moving on up. My parents' first apartment together had been in LeFrak City, Queens. Then they'd moved all the way out to Stony Brook, on eastern Long Island, then Centerport, then Plainview, and now, if they got this house, to Rockville Centre, a town of hardworking Catholics and Jews and Protestants with nationally ranked public schools, a fifteen-minute drive from Jones Beach.

"Our last one, I hope," my mother said. My parents were holding hands as my father drove. My brother Josh and I sat side by side in the backseat. Our older brother, Mark, was away at tennis camp and didn't know we were moving.

They sang along to the radio. Moving meant a clean slate: new neighbors and another chance to be the kind of family my parents wanted to be. They would try harder; they would get along. They loved each other, didn't they? Maybe they could even make friends here. My mother's best friend, Constance, who had two boys my brothers' ages, was back in Stony Brook. Her oldest son—who, like my brother, was named Mark—had developed a dangerously high fever in fifth grade, suffering brain damage. He was permanently altered, mentally retarded, not like the boy in my class at school who was called slow, but much worse off. The two Marks had been playmates as babies when our two families lived next door. Now Mark Stevens was nonverbal and needed to be carried to the toilet. Constance, who was beautiful and kind, had gotten divorced. She was a struggling single mom, and once he got too big to take care of at home, her oldest would need to go live in a special school that sounded more like a hospital. *We* were the lucky ones.

The real estate agent met us in front of the house. Josh and I were impressed. From the curb, we saw a Tudor-style beige and brick house edged with brown, like something out of a storybook. Josh and I unbuckled our lap belts and stepped out of the car.

Could we really afford this?

"It's a stretch," my mother was saying. She'd already seen the house and wanted to show it to my father.

"It's a bit of a fixer-upper," the real estate agent informed him, shaking my father's hand. "But it's a good investment. A property in Rockville Centre will always sell."

"My husband is handy," my mother said. My father knew how to fix things. He was smart, too. He had a Ph.D. in educational psychology and was a researcher at LaGuardia Community College in Long Island City. He drove to work with an ax tucked underneath the seat of his car. He said he needed it *just in case*.

"Marty, you could do the kitchen and the downstairs bathroom yourself."

Climbing three steps to the front door, I walked into the house, which opened onto a narrow entryway with high ceilings and a sparkly fancy-looking chandelier.

"Is that staying?" my mother wanted to know, pointing up.

"Yes," said the agent. "All the fixtures stay."

To the right was a formal living room with wood floors and a real working fireplace, separated by a folding door from the family room behind it. On the left was a dining room that connected to the kitchen with the sort of swinging saloon-style half-doors I'd seen in cowboy movies.

"This will be perfect for Thanksgiving and the Jewish holidays," my mother said, leading my father into the dining room. We usually had my grandmother, my uncle Alan, and his live-in girlfriend, Elaine, over.

Upstairs were the bedrooms, including a double-sized baby-blue room looking onto the street that my brothers could share, and a smaller one with darker blue wallpaper and a view of the backyard. That would be mine.

"Marty, you'll have to paint this room," my mother said, noticing me.

"Eventually," he said.

At the top of the stairs, as if to make up for all that blue, sat a large and unapologetically pink bathroom, with original 1920s tiles and a pedestal sink and toilet and bathtub and a separate shower, for the children to share. On the other side of the second floor was the master bedroom, with two closets, including a large walk-in for my mother, and a private bathroom. This was everything my mother could want.

My father went down to the unfinished basement to inspect the water heater and oil tank and boiler. My mother brought Josh and me to the backyard to show us the very best thing about the house. Could it be? A swimming pool!

But the pool was the problem. My father didn't want one.

"Too much work," he said when he saw it. "And who do you think is going to end up taking care of it?" Perhaps he also pointed out that the humble pool, with a short diving board on one end and a ladder on the other, took up almost the entire yard, with no grass or room for a swing set like we had in Plainview.

The house was a bargain, though. My mother listed the reasons why on her fingers—the schools, the neighborhood, the house itself. She'd be a three-minute drive from work. The closest elementary school was a few blocks away, and the town had two synagogues to choose from.

We would take it.

At the signing, my parents sat on one side of a rectangular conference table, me settled behind them on a chair along the wall with a book. The sellers took the other side. My mother told me that the man who owned the house had made his money at the racetrack. Whether from owning horses or gambling I didn't know, but either way it sounded seedy. Their kids were grown, and they didn't need a house anymore. His belly hung over his belt, pushing it low and at an angle, like my father's belly, only much bigger, making it so he couldn't bring his chair all the way up to the table.

The adults worked their way through the contract papers. But there was one last thing. My father wanted the pool cover thrown in. The owner wanted to charge us for it. The two of them went back and forth, their voices louder with each exchange.

"Give me a break. What the hell do you need a pool cover for?" my father finally said, standing up. He was about to walk out and call the deal off. The owner stood up, too.

When we went out to a restaurant, I worried about my father stiffing a waiter because he wasn't satisfied with the service, or even telling the hostess off. Sometimes it was just a sneer and some cursing. Other times he lost control. Now he looked angry enough to punch the owner, or one of the lawyers or the real estate brokers or the man from the bank, or maybe even me if I didn't stay invisible.

The lawyers on both sides tried to calm their clients. I pretended to read my book.

"Marty," my mother said. "I want this house."

She'd grown up in an apartment in Jackson Heights, Queens. My father was raised in an apartment, too, a tenement, in Washington Heights. The right house, *this* house, would make up for that and everything else that wasn't okay. My mother's material requirements were relatively modest when compared to those of her teacher friends, some of whose husbands made much more than my father did. She wore her diamond engagement ring on one hand and a gold wedding band on the other, and had a jewelry box filled with costume pieces and a few necklaces in sterling silver or the thinnest gold. It wasn't like she demanded fur coats and tennis bracelets. Besides, it was her money, too. She worked.

He sat down. The papers were signed.

Soon boxes filled our old house. I'd say goodbye to my room with the yellow wallpaper. My mother packed my Raggedy Ann doll and my *Mister Rogers Talks About* book and the plastic plates featuring our drawings that my parents had sent away to be made. Mine had green grass and an orange sun and blue sky and my name on top. My brothers drew themselves playing ball. We'd move in time for the school year. Mark and Josh and I would start over again. We all would.

To celebrate, we went to a Chinese restaurant in Rockville Centre and ordered egg rolls, even though they had pork in them, and a dish that came to the table on fire.

"Are we rich?" I asked my father. We didn't usually go to places this nice. We'd have dinner at a restaurant that had sawdust and peanuts on the floor, or on special occasions we'd go to an Italian family-style place where I ordered the meatless manicotti, which came with the baked cheese satisfyingly stuck to the serving dish. But the combination of the Chinese restaurant with a coat check and dim lighting and signed photographs of the Long Island Rangers, plus the house with the swimming pool, made me think things had changed.

"No." He laughed, putting together a moo shu pancake. "We're middle class."

*   *   *

Rockville Centre was the kind of place some people never left, and never wanted to. We were a town of volunteer firefighters, Ash Wednesday observers, Little League teams, and shared bedrooms. In the center of town was the Long Island Rail Road station—thirty-eight or forty-two minutes to Manhattan, depending on the train. The Golden Reef Diner and St. Agnes Cathedral. Not to mention the Fantasy movie theater and Hunan Wok with $4.95 lunch specials and a Woolworth's that sold nail polish and greeting cards. Close to town were a small housing project and some low-rise apartment buildings. From there, neighborhoods of houses ringed out from the town center. Residents of the inner core were solidly middle and working class— policemen and teachers and insurance agents and nurses. In the larger, more expensive homes on the wealthier side of town, fathers were small-business owners and lawyers and the occasional doctor or dentist. Rich parents were in banking. Our neighborhood was right in the middle. Nice houses but close together. The restricted country club with a golf course that didn't let in African-American or Jewish families (other than a rumored one or two) was down the street from my house.

Some mothers worked, but some didn't, and their kids got to go home for lunch during the school day. After staying home with my brothers and me, my mother had been working part-time as a reading specialist since I was two, but now she was teaching study skills as part of a high school English department, and she hoped to be assigned regular English classes down the line. She subscribed to *Ms.* and *Working Mother*. At the supermarket checkout counter, she'd grab *Good Housekeeping* and *Ladies' Home Journal,* too. (When I was old enough to decipher it, I'd pore over the *LHJ* "Can This Marriage Be Saved?" column, not knowing whether to pray for my parents to stay together or break up.) Some semesters she'd take an education course at a local college and be gone one or two evenings a week. At the start of a term, she collated reading packets on the dining room table. She had a closet full of teacher clothes—skirts with forgiving elastic waistbands and matching tops, culottes and wrap dresses, and the occasional pair of dungarees for Fridays. Lots of Liz Claiborne. Underneath she wore padded and pointy B-cup bras, and underpants that came almost as high as her belly button, covering the swell of her tummy. Twice a year she bought a new pocketbook. She collected "ethnic" jewelry.

As a full-time working mom, she didn't usually have the time or energy for spaghetti and meatballs or taco night or breaded chicken cutlets or hot dogs or hamburgers with frozen french fries or frozen string beans or peas on the side, like she used to. It became easier to boil water for pasta shells and leave an open can of tomato sauce on the counter. (I hated meat, anyway.) She went to Weight Watchers meetings and ate turkey burgers without the bun and frozen yogurt for dessert. She hardly ever drank. She read contemporary fiction, favoring women writers, and had a paperback copy of *Dianetics*. She tried to remember to say *sugar* instead of *shit*. She wasn't affectionate or touchy-feely, though she did like it when I gave her foot massages, and sometimes she'd scratch letters into my back and let me guess them. Her skin was smooth. Her nose was ruler-straight. She dyed her hair in the sink and hung her control-top panty hose over the towel rack. She was thirty-six.

Weekday mornings, while he listened to Don Imus on the radio, my father got out the cereal, Cap'n Crunch or Frosted Flakes or Raisin Bran, and if my mother didn't have time for my braids or barrettes, he did my hair himself. Mark took the bus or rode his bike to middle school. Josh and I walked, or got a ride from our father when the weather was bad. We were on our own in the afternoons until our mother came home. When I was old enough, I'd wear a house key on a loop around my neck and let myself in. For now, my brothers were in charge. Josh, who was in fifth grade, walked me home from school, and afterward he and Mark, who was in seventh, took absentminded care of me, heating us up Ellio's pizza in the toaster oven before running off with their friends to play catch or basketball in the driveway, or Ping-Pong in the basement, or, later on, poker in their bedroom.

In Ms. Doctor's second-grade class at Wilson Elementary, I was the new kid, and I wasn't sporty and preppy like the

Waspy girls, or freckled and spunky like the Catholic girls, or doted on and indulged like some of the other Jewish children. I was growing out a Dorothy Hamill haircut, and my unruly hair would never fall straight past my shoulders. Plus, I'd become chubby. Pleasantly plump, my father said. A cute, mean boy named Mike called me "Bubble Burger" and got some of the other boys to call me that, too. Dave G. broke my pencil right in the middle of class, and my teacher said it was because he had a crush on me, but even though he had red hair and glasses, I knew that couldn't be true. A boy named Val wouldn't stop calling me names.

I told my parents, who told Josh to teach Val a lesson. It happened on the way home from school, right where kids and the crossing guard could see. Val started taunting me, and Josh told him to shut up. When he wouldn't, my brother punched him. Val was tough, but only for a second-grader. Josh was older. Self-defense, my mother called it. My parents were certain we'd done the right thing, even though my mom could get in trouble because she taught in the same school district. You had to stick up for yourself. *You couldn't go like a lamb to the slaughter.*

Josh was my hero, my mother said when my brother returned from school with blood on his shirt and a note from the principal. "Thank your brother!" she instructed me.

*   *   *

But at least my parents were home each night, packing lunches and making sure we had clean laundry and school supplies. My father chaperoned my class field trips (the only dad who did), and when I was younger, he gave me piggyback rides high up on his shoulders. If I needed something xeroxed for class, I left it on top of his briefcase. He sat on the couch with his sewing kit during *60 Minutes* and stitched up the loose neck of my stuffed Sherlock Holmes dog, pretending he was a dog doctor. When I was sick, he moved a television into my room. In the summers, he put an air conditioner in my bedroom window and let me blast it, even though it was expensive to run.

He took me to a dance store to buy ballet slippers, and we left with a pink pair that fit just right, and a wisp of a dance skirt in black, and two leotards. One time my father let my brothers and me come to his office on a school holiday, and I ran and slipped in my rain boots. Blood poured everywhere. *Fuck,* he said, racing me to the car and carrying me in his arms like a baby. The emergency room doctor said I needed a dozen stitches on my forehead, right below where my scalp met my hairline. My father held me down and whispered reassurances into my ear as the doctor sewed me up.

Of course, I never talked about *it* with my father. I'd never dare.

A day or two after hurting me, my father would approach me with a wordless apology. He'd bring home Chinese takeout for dinner. My mother got her favorite egg rolls. He'd ladle extra wontons into my soup. We'd eat our chow mein. And fried rice, too—a splurge, since white rice came free with the meal. He'd caress my cheek with the back of his hand.

You're my favorite, he'd whisper.
I turned to him like a dying plant turns to sunshine.
You're the apple of my eye. You're my sheyne meydele.

* * *

And so afterward, when it was all over, we pretended nothing had happened. We went back to normal. I pushed down my fear. I acted like I was fine. I sat in synagogue wearing a drop-waist Gunne Sax dress. I worked on my poetry report. I studied the words on my spelling list and let my mother quiz me on them. My father made my mother a dinner salad with boiled eggs and baby potatoes and lots of oil and vinegar and garlic powder. On Sunday mornings he cooked up home fries and omelets or chocolate-chip pancakes. He told me I was smart and special.

My mother never spoke of the violence in our house, which made me think I might be crazy. Though some days, after she came home from her new job, I found her sitting on the toilet in her bathroom upstairs, crying, with fistfuls of wadded-up toilet paper. I didn't ask why. Other times she was sick or had a crushing headache or felt faint and hypoglycemic and would call in for a sub and spend the day in bed, and we weren't to disturb her. Maybe she hated herself for not being brave enough to leave him. Maybe she thought he would change. But for the most part she was stoic and stony and seemed resigned to her life.

Once, when I was five, our parents saved up and found cheap tickets and took my brothers and me on a dreamlike trip to Spain and Portugal. We visited castles and climbed up winding stone staircases through ancient turrets. During breakfasts on the patio at small family inns, my brothers and I ran and played on the grass while our parents drank their café con leche, and we ate dinners together at outdoor restaurants as the sun set, way past our bedtimes. At a bullfight, I made my family walk out because I couldn't stand to watch the gore, to hear the crowd cheering as the matador pushed his sticks into the bull. One afternoon my mother lingered in a shop in Madrid and bought two embroidered silk shawls and delicate lace-trimmed fans, one for her and one for me. Even though my father got pissed off when he couldn't find his way around the city, and screamed at my mother when we almost missed our ferry in Portugal, that shawl and fan became for me treasured totems, representing all my family could be.

Proof that I wasn't crazy or making all the bad things up were the planets of black and blue up and down my arms and legs and across my back. My father marked my body. He stamped me. A few times he even made me bleed, but never enough that I needed to go to the doctor. He never gave me a black eye or a broken bone, nothing that would alarm my mother's teacher friends and make them call child welfare services. The bright imprint of his slaps on my cheeks always burned off by the time I was ready to go to school the next day. It's possible no adult ever noticed anything.

My parents said I bruised easily. They said I was clumsy. And it was true that I bumped into edges and angles of household furniture that others might maneuver with a thoughtless grace. I was anxious in that house. When I knocked into something, a reminder of the accident would almost instantly appear on my pale skin. Too sensitive, my parents said.

Small things worried me. My mother asked me how many times a day I changed my underpants. Once, I answered, having never thought about this question. She said I should be changing twice at a minimum, in the morning and at night. Sometimes she changed hers in the afternoon, too, she told me. She was only trying to teach me things, but I felt stupid and dirty. It was difficult for me to have a sense of proportion.

There were times when I was happy. Roller-skating to a good song at Hot Skates. Riding my bike. Pumping myself high on the swings at the elementary school playground. I made wishes. On the way home from school, I sang "Maybe" from *Annie* to myself. I jumped on certain crispy leaves and wouldn't step on sidewalk cracks. I hoped things would change.

TWO

ON THE WAY to Maine, my brothers and I took turns stretching out in the "back back" of our father's 1976 blue Toyota Corolla station wagon. Mark was five years older than I was. Joshua—Josh—the middle child, was three years older, and then there was me, Jessie. It would have been August. My father, Martin—Marty to my mom, Daddy to me—was at the wheel, and my mother, Sheila, sat beside him in the passenger seat. Mark and Josh passed Mad Libs back and forth. We counted how many different state license plates we could spot during the drive from Long Island to the cabin our parents had rented on Rangeley Lake. We played the geography game.

"Alabama," my dad suggested.

"Alaska!" I shouted, proud to be the littlest and still right.

"Arkansas," said Mark.

"This is boring," said Josh.

Even though Mark and Josh fought sometimes, they shared a room, baseball bats and catchers' mitts, a Boy Scout troop, and a gang of neighborhood friends. Our mother wasn't the sort to play with us. She'd read to me or take me clothes shopping. She'd even taken me into the city a couple of times to see a Broadway show. But she wasn't there to entertain me, or to be my friend, and she told me as much. My father was the one who liked to spend time with me, who cared about what I thought and enjoyed the way my brain worked.

"Let's play twenty questions," Daddy said, knowing this was my favorite car game.

"Is it bigger than a bread box?" I asked.

Back then his hair was more pepper than salt, and he sported a reddish-brown mustache that tickled when he kissed me. My mother tried to get him to shave it off, but he wouldn't. He wasn't vain, but he was determined and intractable, stubborn about doing things his way. On warm-weather weekends and summer vacation days like this, he wore old plaid Bermuda shorts and white tube socks stretched taut all the way from his sneakers to his dry, flaky knees. He had on thick-framed glasses, a velour short-sleeve shirt with a generous late-seventies collar, and his aqua fishing cap with a leaping fish on the front and mesh on the sides. With the steering wheel in one hand, he balanced a thermos of coffee in the other, putting it down between his legs or handing it over to my mother to hold when he needed to use the stick shift. She couldn't drive a stick, but this model had been cheaper.

By the time we pulled up to a Howard Johnson's for dinner, it was getting late, and we were all starving. The hostess grabbed the oversize laminated adult menus and the smaller, paper children's ones from the stand and showed us to our table. I slid into the booth closest to the window, and the backs of my sweaty thighs stuck to the vinyl. I got to draw on my menu with the restaurant crayons, and after dinner we were allowed to have ice cream for dessert because it came free with the meal. Then it was time to climb back into the car for the final push to the cabin.

Mark let me rest my head on his lap, and I curled my legs up underneath myself so that I could lie down. It was getting late. Out the window I could see the summer sun setting and the sky turning dark blue and then black as the stars appeared. The moon followed us. We turned off the highway, where we could smell the sea, onto country roads, passing general stores and seafood shacks until I fell asleep and we made our way inland. My father must have carried me in from the car slung over his shoulder. I woke up early the next morning, tucked under a sleeping bag on the lower level of a bunk bed, needing to pee. The log cabin reminded me of the Lincoln Log sets my brothers sometimes built.

The days passed peacefully. My father was happy in Maine, which was why. We went to sleep by nightfall, and I stirred when the light came in under the children's bedroom door. My father would have put water on for instant Folgers before setting out early into the cool, misty morning in his mustard-yellow flannel shirt and Wrangler jeans, heading to the lake with his tackle box, my brothers following close behind.

My grandmother, my mother's mother, was in the cabin with my mom and me. She must have driven up from her apartment in Queens. She and I played cards, war and crazy eights and go fish, on the screened-in porch while my mother read. After lunch, we'd all go for a swim. The bottom of the shallowest part of the lake was mushy and rocky and pebbly all at once, and algae jammed between my toes. I could see tiny fish swimming all around me. I stayed in the water, wading, while my brothers practiced their jumps off the dock. "Watch *me,* Mommy," I said.

Back at the cabin, I peeled off my swimsuit, and my mother took out her bottle of calamine lotion and smeared the pink cream on my mosquito bites. I had more than anyone else in the family. Dozens. "That's because you're the sweetest," my father said.

The night before our last full day of the trip, I begged to go fishing, too. Why should I always be left behind just because I was a girl? I'd listened to my *Free to Be You and Me* album so many times the record had warped, and I knew that wasn't fair. Besides, it was boring to always be stuck with my mother and grandmother, to miss out on all the adventures the boys got to have.

My father agreed. He said he'd teach me how to put a worm on a hook. I'd be his first mate, his special helper.

"Marty," my mother said with a tone of warning in her voice. "She doesn't know how to swim. It's too deep. It's way too dangerous."

"She'll wear a life jacket," he replied in a tone of his own that said, *What I say goes, and that's final.* Which meant I could come.

The next morning he woke me up early, and we walked down to the rowboat fitted with a small outboard motor rented for our stay. I sat in the middle row, wearing my borrowed salmon-colored life preserver. My father let me help paddle for a while, until he started the motor. After what seemed like a long time but was probably no more than five or ten minutes, he killed the motor and reached for the can of worms resting in a puddle by my feet, grabbing a live one for his rod and one for each of my brothers' rods. His thick fingers nimbly curved the wriggly worms through the hooks. He should have been a surgeon, he said, or at least a plumber. Should have worked with his hands. Should have made money. I was little but already familiar with his regrets.

We were quiet on the boat, waiting for something to happen. I pulled my sweatshirt around my bare legs to stay warm.

My father got the first tug. "We have one. Come over here," he said. "Feel this."

He placed my hands on the rod under his, and I felt the pull, the force of the fish fighting back for life. Daddy dug his feet into the sides of the boat and reeled in his catch. By morning's end, we had three fish flopping on the bottom of the boat. Not bad. It was sunny now, and hot. I stripped off my sweatshirt and shorts and wore just a one-piece bathing suit under my life vest. I ran my fingers through the water next to me, letting them glide and float and create ripples. We ate our tuna and peanut butter and jelly sandwiches, and then my father said it was time to drive around the lake some more and for my brothers to have a swim. He turned on the motor and we went fast, making a sharp path through the dark blue water, white surf misting my face. We came to a stop. Josh jumped like a cannonball, and Mark dove in, while my father stayed on the boat with me. For a few minutes my brothers circled us, swimming freestyle, showing off with the breast- or sidestroke, or back-floating when they got tired.

They must have decided to swim out a bit. Maybe they were having a race. Or maybe we'd simply begun to drift, or they did, or maybe it just looked to me like the space kept widening between my father and me in the boat and my brothers in the water.

"How deep is the water here?" I asked my father.

"Maybe a hundred feet? I'm not sure. Very deep," he said.

As my brothers receded from view, I became more and more nervous, and my father was worried, too. My mother's warnings clanged in my head. My brothers were good swimmers, but they were young, and we were in the middle of a vast lake. I imagined the lakebed to be the very bottom of Earth. An inconceivable distance away, like space itself, only in the opposite direction. Would I ever see my brothers again?

This was like a game we played in the family room back at home, where the couch was a ship and the carpet was the water and there were sharks, and as long as you were in the water, you weren't safe. You had to get back to the couch/ship. But this was for real. I started to cry. "Come back!" I hollered.

Josh started teasing me, swimming even farther away. Mark was my protector, but Josh was close enough to my

age to torment me. They couldn't have been very far from the boat at all, but it felt like they were.

"Get back in this boat *now,*" my father yelled. He was angry. His skin was turning red and blotchy. My brothers began swimming back in our direction, exhausted and out of breath, able to manage just a doggy-paddle toward the end.

But it was too late. Even though they were inches from us, my father was furious. As Josh treaded water and tried to explain himself, my father grabbed the wooden oar off the boat and, reaching down to my brother in the lake, smacked him with it squarely across the body. The blow was brutal in its purposefulness. Josh's howl echoed on the lake, skimming the surface of the water. My brothers climbed back in the boat and shivered under a shared towel. And then there was nothing but still water. We were as quiet as we'd been when fishing, only now the silence rang in my ears. We motored home without saying a word. I never told my mother what happened, and I wouldn't discuss it with my brothers, or anyone else, for twenty years.

That afternoon we fried up the fish in an iron pan for a snack. We showered off, and my mother rinsed out my hair with No More Tears baby shampoo, and we all dressed up and went to a lobster dinner in town. I had on a white and navy sailor dress. There were homemade dinner rolls in a basket, and packets of butter. My mother covered my dress with two cloth napkins on my lap and a plastic bib over my chest. She showed me how to crack open the lobster claw and reach in for the meat with a tiny fork. My father didn't say much. His anger lingered like a hangover.

*   *   *

One weekend my father and I were watching *The Life and Times of Grizzly Adams,* a show about an innocent man on the run from the law who takes to the wilderness and befriends a bear. I thought about running away all the time. Sometimes I daydreamed about opening a dog hotel. Or living in New York City with artsy divorced parents who'd learn to become friends, like in my favorite Norma Klein novels. Then I'd have to see my father (though he wouldn't exactly be my father but a calmer Alan Alda type) only on the weekends, and I was pretty sure we could get along then.

During the commercials, a public service announcement came on the television. A boy with sandy-blond hair and a dirty T-shirt stood in a dimly lit alley. The announcer spoke: "It shouldn't hurt to be a child. Stop child abuse before it starts." A hotline number flashed, disappearing before I could memorize it.

I didn't dare look at my father. I didn't dare move a muscle. My skin was on fire. *That was me!* I knew that much for sure. But I didn't know what it meant. Should I call that hotline after school, when my brothers were playing catch in the driveway? And if I did, what would happen? Would a social worker with her gray hair in a bun show up at my door one day, carrying a clipboard with my name on it? Would my father go to jail? Did I want him to? (And if he did, what would he do to me when he got out?) I considered keeping a pencil and paper hidden

in the family room so that the next time the commercial came on, I'd be ready and could take down the number, but the truth was, I couldn't decide if I wanted my father to get into trouble.

How could I explain to a judge and jury the complicated ways in which some of our best moments as a family were knotted together with some of our most shameful ones?

*   *   *

Another summer came. My father was talking on the kitchen phone, excitedly jotting notes on a pad of paper. Something was up.

"Sheila!" he said as soon as he hung up the receiver.

A summer camp had called. An expensive Jewish sleep-away camp in the Catskill Mountains, the kind my parents couldn't afford, where kids packed trunks with Izod shirts and days-of-the-week underwear from Bloomingdale's, all with their name tags sewn in or ironed on. Where parents mailed weekly goody bags gift-wrapped at fancy stationery and candy stores. After a last-minute staffing cancellation, an old acquaintance of my father's had phoned to see if my parents might be interested in coming up for the summer to work as unit heads. The July session was beginning in a few weeks. They wouldn't get paid very much, but my brothers and I would get to attend the camp for free.

"Where will we stay?" my mother wanted to know. No way was she going to sleep in a bunk with her charges, she said. "I look forward to my summers all year long. I am *not* going to be a glorified camp counselor."

"Don't be such a prude," he answered. "It's like getting thousands of dollars in camp tuition for free, and the boys will love it."

"What about Jessie?" Yeah, what about me? I wondered. I was pretty certain I wasn't old enough for sleepaway camp, even if my parents were nearby.

"She'll be fine."

My brothers and I were in the kitchen, following the debate like one of Mark's tennis matches. My mother put her hands on her hips.

"We're going," my father said.

"Upstairs." She pointed Mark, Josh, and me to our bedrooms. "Now."

Since this was all last-minute, they had to tell the camp that day. My brothers let me sit in their room while our parents fought.

By the time we were called down to eat, she'd finally agreed. But later, after my father phoned back and accepted, he revealed more of the details. From what I could gather, he had initially made it seem like the job would be administrative, when really they'd be working directly with counselors and young campers.

"You lied to me," she said when she found out. "You're going to pay for this."

"It's too late," he said smugly. "We're going."

A few weeks later, we loaded up the car. We left early in the morning, because my parents had to be there for staff orientation. My mother was coming, but she was *not happy about it,* and sat with a magazine on her lap, flipping through the pages.

She and I had spent the days since school ended making our way through the long camp checklist for girls. We'd needed to gather a summer camp trousseau: seven to ten pairs of shorts, ten T-shirts, sweatpants and sweatshirts and long-sleeve shirts, twelve pairs of underwear, two or three bathing suits and six towels, a flashlight, and an assortment of other summer camp paraphernalia. That morning I put on a new outfit and fixed my hair in a high ponytail. Out the car window, I saw the organized houses and lawns of our town turn to bridges and tree-lined highways and then the hills of the lower Catskills.

We reached the camp, parked, and got out to have a look around. There was green everywhere. Josh and Mark wanted to run to the lake. First things first, our mother said. She wanted to see where she'd be sleeping. It wasn't as bad as she'd imagined. They'd have a tiny but quaint one-room cabin just big enough for a double bed and dresser, a short walk from the campers and counselors they'd be supervising. Pacified, my mother helped me unpack my things and arrange them into neat piles in my cubby. That night I'd sleep in the bunk with my new counselors. The next day, the rest of the campers would arrive.

When camp began, I was on my own for the first time ever. Part of me liked being separated from my parents, sleeping in a bed far from them. I wanted to feel carefree. But what I really felt was scared to be alone, and more afraid than ever that we'd be found out. It seemed dangerous to let my father live among all of these strangers. While making key-chain lanyards and ceramics and trying to get out of swimming lessons, I worried. During meals, I waved to my parents on the other side of the dining hall and drank as much bug juice as I wanted. I ran into my brothers at the canteen or during Friday-night services by the lake, but mostly, when not in activity after activity, I sat on my bed reading, or on the porch, impressing the other young campers with my ability to forecast the rain by my headaches. At night, I cried myself to sleep. I didn't know why. A counselor came over and rubbed my back. She wanted to know what was wrong. I couldn't say. I couldn't even explain it to myself.

A week or two into the eight-week summer, the counselor woke me in what felt like the middle of the night. A cool hand on my arm, a gentle shake. My mother was waiting for me on the porch.

"We're leaving," she said, her arms crossed against her chest. She shushed me when I tried to ask what was wrong. "Pack your clothes. Don't let anyone hear you. And do *not* wake anybody up."

"Now?" I asked. I didn't know if it was closer to bedtime or morning.

Mark and Josh and my father were waiting in the car. Nobody said a word. My mother handed my brothers and me a banana each. They didn't explain why we had to leave. Mark and Josh were pissed. I was mostly confused. I wondered whether we were going home because I cried in the

middle of the night, or because my mother really was a prude
and a priss, like my father said. But then we drove away
before the camp woke up, without saying goodbye to the
other campers or counselors, which made me think we *had*
to leave. I could only imagine my father had done something
wrong, something shameful. Or who knows, maybe they
quit. Maybe my mother decided to stand up to him just this
once, when it counted the very least. I never did find out.

*   *   *

My father was offered a research job at a university upstate.
SUNY Oswego, I think. The five of us drove up to check
out the town. Out the window, I saw cows and horses. The
country! My mother pointed out two smokestacks in the
distance and the swath of gray sky as we rode closer to
the college.

"Where will they go to Hebrew school?" she asked my
father from the passenger seat. "The nearest temple is an
hour away."

He turned down the job. We remained on Long Island
and adopted a dog from the animal shelter, a shaggy and
sweet mutt. (Our old dog had died back in Plainview.)
Snoopy would sniff my hair and play catch with a tennis
ball and go swimming in the pool, jumping off the side and
doggy-paddling to fetch the ball, shaking water off his back
as he climbed the ladder to get out. We just walked him
around the block for a few minutes two or three times a
day to pee and poop, and so every once in a while he'd run

away, free, upending the neighborhood garbage cans and roaming through back alleys toward the expanse of shared green grass on the other side of our fence.

When Mark was about to start high school, it sank in that my mother would be teaching in the same building, and he packed an old steamer trunk we had in the garage and wheeled it over to his friend's house. My parents let him stay the night. We all knew Mark had every right to be upset. Having your mother teach in your school was embarrassing and unfair, and it was something we'd all have to go through eventually. The next day, after our father went to pick Mark up, our parents said he could move a bed into the attic, Greg Brady–style, and take a small black-and-white TV with him. He lasted just a few weeks up there. Fall came and the attic wasn't heated. And he missed Josh. But his aborted attempt at freedom made an impression on me. Sometimes I'd pretend to run away, too, tying a red bandanna to a stick and taking Snoopy for a walk and playing hobo.

My brothers were getting too old to be hit, or maybe they were better behaved than I was, or maybe my father liked them more because they were boys, or maybe it was simply easier to hit a girl. Josh and Mark would play ball in the driveway for hours with a baseball and bat. They'd play basketball using a hoop attached to the front of the garage. Sometimes my father would join them. Snoopy would be tied on a leash to the chain-link fence between the driveway and pool. My brothers usually knew how to stay out of the worst trouble. But one day, out of nowhere, my father was chasing Josh and Mark through the house. I don't know what started this particular argument, but I was in my room when I heard him roaring. I felt relieved that it wasn't me this time and guilty for feeling that way. Then they were across the hall in my brothers' bedroom. I stayed put but watched through the few inches of my cracked-open door. My father was beating them up like a schoolyard bully, giving each boy a turn as they cried out. He had one of them on the ground and was holding him down. One brother, I can't remember which one, fought back. I never fought back.

They were athletes. Not just in the driveway. They played on basketball and baseball and tennis teams. I watched them from the bleachers. They were *boys,* I thought. They were lucky. They would outgrow him, I realized that day, but I never would. He'd always be bigger than me. What would happen if the three of us, Mark and Josh and me, came together and turned on him? An insurrection, a revolt—maybe we didn't even need our mother. Surely the three of us could take him on. If not right away, then one day.

Because when our parents' arguments escalated, when the yelling wouldn't stop, when it became unbearably bad, we did come together. A threesome at last, we watched from the upstairs landing, huddled together with Mark's protective arms slung over our shoulders.

He was calling her names. She was a *stupid bitch*. Like me. She cried out in fear, trying to escape him. *"Marty, don't!"*

33

We saw him slam her against the peeling yellow of the refrigerator. Hard.

She started crying harder; I knew that would only make him angrier.

He threw his arm up, a threat and a promise.

"No!" she cried. I heard the fear in her voice. Like she was afraid for her life. Not that he would kill her, but that all she knew and depended on would collapse around her.

"IN YOUR ROOMS! NOW!" our father thundered, catching us watching him.

We hid in Mark and Josh's room, not nearly brave enough to stay for what came next. Did he hit her? Did he slap her? We heard yelling and screaming and the sound of hurled objects and then the deadly quiet, but I couldn't be certain.

Mark locked the door and got out his record albums, and we played *Sergeant Pepper's* and *The Wall* and Billy Joel's *The Stranger* and *52nd Street* and *Glass Houses,* turning the volume all the way up on the stereo that he'd bought with his own money. We stayed up there for hours. I sat on Mark's bed. The three of us let Billy Joel and Pink Floyd do the talking.

Later on, when my mother said that my brothers and I could only rely on one another, it was those moments that made me think she was right.

* * *

My father only left once.

"I'm done," he said. I stood in the doorway of their bedroom and watched him throw an old suitcase at the foot of their bed, grabbing clothes and a toothbrush and his round plastic military comb. It was a Sunday night, and he'd been shouting at my mother for over an hour. But now he ignored her, which worried me even more.

"You've never paid a bill in your life," he said. "Good luck."

The bedroom door slammed behind him. Then we heard his car starting up. He peeled out of our driveway. We were alone, abandoned. My mother was crying. We'd lose the house. What would we do? Where would we go? I pictured us at a battered-women's shelter.

The next day he came home from work like nothing had happened.

*   *   *

I couldn't make myself stop hating my parents. So instead, I wanted to make everything stop. I fantasized about slitting my wrists. I imagined slicing them with a knife in the bathtub, where I would sink down into the warmth of blood and bubbles. I liked to picture myself floating away.

But the truth was, I avoided physical risk and injury. I never broke an arm or leg or sprained an ankle. I went on one rec-center ski trip and clung to the bunny slope's rope pull and never went back. I quit gymnastics when we had to practice backbends; I didn't go out for soccer or any other team sport. I couldn't manage the monkey bars. I stayed close to the rails during ice-skating lessons. I resented dodgeball in gym class. I hated getting hurt. I didn't even like to make my muscles sore.

During recess, instead of playing kickball with the other kids, I'd sit on a tree stump and read. Reading was my version of running away. I read the *Anne of Green Gables* series and *The Good Earth* and *Little Women* and *Heidi* and *Jane Eyre*. I read all of the Judy Blume books (sneaking *Forever . . .*, which my mother forbid), *Are You There God? It's Me, Margaret,* and *Blubber* and *Then Again, Maybe I Won't,* and Norma Klein novels like *Mom, The Wolfman and Me,* even though my mother said I wasn't really old enough for them. I heard about psychoanalysis and started seeing any willing children in my class as "patients" for my idea of therapy sessions. I found an out-of-date appointment book in the attic, created homemade Rorschach inkblot tests, and asked my classmate-clients to remember and bring me their dreams. I kept a journal by my bed and wrote down mine.

I loved Mister Rogers when I was young, because he liked me for me. Once I got older, I graduated to *Happy Days* and *The Brady Bunch* and *Eight Is Enough* and especially *Little House on the Prairie,* which my mother would sometimes watch with me. I sat in front of the TV hour after hour, watching the easy way family conflicts could develop and be resolved in an episode. I identified with Laura because she was brave, and her family had more than its fair share of hardships, even though my father was no Pa. On Saturday nights, when my parents went out to dinner parties or restaurants, I got to eat a TV dinner and stay up late and watch all night long. First *Solid Gold* and then *The Love Boat* and even *Fantasy Island,* which my mother said was also too mature for me.

Just like my mother did, I worried about my weight, even as I snacked on potato chips and rocky-road ice cream while watching TV or reading before bed. On weigh-in day at school, the girls in my fifth-grade class lined up in the nurse's office and climbed on the doctor's scale one by one, the nurse announcing our weight as she marked the number on a Presidential Fitness form. When it was my turn, she had to slide the top metal marker almost all the way to the right. I was one of the shortest children in class but weighed more than almost any of the other girls: 88 pounds, or 93, or maybe it was 97. I was old enough to know how ashamed I should be, how wrong my body was, how only adults thought I was cute. When my mother took me to Chwatsky's, a clothing store we couldn't afford, she had to get me a size fourteen, just like Josh had to wear husky jeans, just like my mother had to go to the plus-size department for herself when she wasn't being good. My weight was the most disgusting thing about me, or so I thought, and everyone could see it.

When my birthday came, my mother took me to the pediatrician for my annual physical. We made the trip all the time. I missed a lot of school. I had a steady stream of sore throats and ear infections, and the doctors were always willing to prescribe me the bottle of sticky pink penicillin my mother wanted for me, even though they told her I didn't really need it, I had a virus, that was all, *but if it made my mother feel better* . . .

When the nurse had me step on the scale, I took my shoes off, and my mother pretended to look away. But when we sat together in the doctor's office after the exam, he brought up the number. It was important to be active, he said. Perhaps I could join a sports team or go back to gymnastics.

"Is there anything else I can do for you today?" he asked, looking at me.

I had those black and blue marks along my arms and legs, and the headaches that had me vomiting in the nurse's office at school, and I hated myself so much I wanted to die.

"I get headaches," I said. "They're really bad." I wanted him to make my mother leave the room. I wanted him to demand that I tell him what was really going on at home. Instead he looked away and checked his watch.

"I'm afraid there's nothing we can do for those," he said. "Take Tylenol."

"I can't swallow a pill," I said.

"Chewable baby aspirin." He nodded to my mother. "She can take four at a time."

THREE

I STOOD HIGH on my tiptoes and reached up to a shelf above
the television to pull down a cream-colored album filled
with luxuriously thick pages of photographs. Sitting on the
family room couch, the nubby blue fabric digging into my
bare legs, I carefully studied the images. I could spend hours
sinking my feet into the shag carpet while looking through
the handful of photo albums my mother had compiled of
our babyhoods and birthdays and family trips, but I prized
this, my parents' wedding album, most of all.

Here, like magic, was my mother, elegant and easy at
twenty-one in her gown and 1960s flip hairdo, and my father,
twenty-two, looking dashing and hopeful in his tuxedo and
more handsome than I'd ever seen him.

They had met as counselors at a summer program for
inner-city kids. I was proud of this fact and pretended it
meant they'd been activists or hippies, even though my
mother explained that they'd been too old for that and that
she'd worn poodle skirts and penny loafers with real pennies in them during high school. So it was more like *Happy
Days*. They could have been beatniks, she said, but they

weren't. She'd listened to Simon and Garfunkel, not Bob Dylan. She'd never smoked a cigarette, much less a joint, or had sex with anyone but my father, and not until they were engaged. For her freshman year, she'd ventured upstate to Elmira College, where she was assigned to room with two of the other Jewish girls on campus. She left after one semester, returning home to be with my father and study at Queens College. Back then, she said, women (like her) had three career options: nurse, secretary, or teacher. My grandmother was a secretary. My mother became a teacher.

My parents were married at a wedding hall in December 1964. In a photograph taken before the ceremony, my mother applied lipstick in the mirror while the train of her modest ivory gown spread out on the floor, encircling her. She wore long white gloves with buttons leading up to her elbows. My father had dark shiny hair, a smart, knowing smile, and was dressed in white tie with tails and a top hat. She must have thought him a catch. He was an Ivy League–educated Jewish boy who loved her. Later I would wonder how much she knew, and had already accepted, going into the marriage. Perhaps she'd never witnessed his temper when they were dating. Or maybe she'd figured she could soften him. Or maybe, at twenty-one, she thought that was just how men were. I imagine what she wanted most of all was to leave home, to live with her boyfriend and spend the night in his arms without her mother or anyone else saying she was a hussy or accusing her of living in sin. In the reception photos, my parents stood smiling behind tables of fashionable-looking guests. I could practically hear the sound of half-full wineglasses tinkling and smell the cigarette smoke. At the end of the night, my mother waved good-bye in front of their rented limo in a Jackie Kennedy–style traveling suit. They spent their wedding night at a hotel in Manhattan and honeymooned in Bermuda.

I recognized few of the guests. Even many of the people under the chuppah, the wedding canopy, were unfamiliar to me. I knew, of course, my maternal grandmother, Kay. She lived in a tidy one-bedroom in Douglaston, Queens, and wore lipstick and eyebrow pencil and carried a compact in her purse. When I was a girl, she hung out at the Jewish Y. She danced the cha-cha and the hora with her best friend, from whom she was inseparable, because there weren't enough men to go around. (My brothers and I whispered other, more romantic theories.) On Fridays, Kay went to the beauty parlor and had her hair washed and set. Every other Sunday she drove to see us on Long Island, bringing babka or black and white cookies or a chocolate cake from the bakery, packaged in a white box tied with red string. Or else my mother and brothers and I went to her apartment and were careful not to break anything. Somehow, between her savings and social security, she had enough money to travel with her Y friends to places as far off as China. She brought me a small porcelain doll from each country they visited. I had a whole shelf of them. But when she came to our house, she sat on the sofa with a grim, sour expression, every so often making a racist comment under her breath about "the shvartzes"—African-Americans she didn't know or care to know.

Her husband, my grandpa Jack, stood next to her in the photos. He died when I was a toddler, before I was old enough to remember him. My mother didn't like to talk about her father. Jack and Kay were separated on and off after my mother left home, and they weren't living together when he died. My grandmother would sometimes come and stay with us, I knew. I'd heard just a few things about my grandfather, none of them good. He was a lawyer but didn't earn a decent living, could never keep his clients, and ended up going bankrupt; he had diabetes and needed to have a toe cut off because he wouldn't take his insulin. There must have been more to the story to make my grandmother keep leaving, given how traditional she was, but mostly what I'd gathered was that my grandfather was what my mother would call a no-goodnik.

My mother's younger brother, Alan, stood under the chuppah, too. He was the rebel in the family, but all that meant was he was a gym teacher who wore bell-bottoms and had hair that came to his collar in the back. He was thin and in shape and had a weak stomach and a series of attractive girlfriends, and he talked about moving to California, but my mother and grandmother warned him about the dangers of earthquakes, so instead he stayed in Queens. At the wedding he would have been eighteen or nineteen.

On the other side of the photographs, to the rabbi's left, was a small lady with curly gray hair. That was my paternal grandmother, Rifka, or Ruth, whose name I was given as my middle name. We didn't have many photographs of Ruth: only the ones in the wedding album and a few of her holding baby Mark in her lap, taken shortly before she died. My father's eyes wet when he saw these. He loved and missed his mother terribly.

Standing next to Ruth was a tall, imposing man, perhaps in his late twenties; a large lady with her dark hair in a beehive; and with them, a young boy and girl a few years apart in age. She was the flower girl, with a basket of rose petals, he the ring bearer, carrying a silk pillow with the two gold bands. Who *were* these people? I didn't know any of them. Why were they under the chuppah? And what about the wedding guests? My parents had pointed out only two or three friends from as many tables.

Just then my father walked in the room.

"Daddy," I asked, not as carefully as I might have, "who are these people with you and Mommy? This man and woman here, and this flower girl and little boy? And the people at these tables?" I pointed first to the ceremony pages and then to the guests at the reception afterward, the women with their short dresses and bouffant blowouts and the men with their smooth haircuts and trim suits.

"Old friends, mostly. People from high school and college we're not in touch with anymore," he said with a vague wave of his hands at the lot of them. "Most of them are dead by now."

My parents were hardly forty. But I believed him.

*　　*　　*

43

One summer day I was in the basement, busy playing with my Fisher-Price schoolhouse and farm and gas station and parking lot and airplane, and my assortment of Little People (the cowboy, the baby, the farmer, the teacher), when I overheard my mother on the phone in the laundry room.

"Marty's sister called," I heard her say. *Sister?* My father was an only child. That was a fact. An only child and an orphan, he'd told me so a million times. His mother died before I was born; his father died when my father was just a boy. He had no family left at all. We were it. We were all he had. *We* were his family. What did she mean, sister? I figured I couldn't have heard right.

Several days later my parents sat me down at our wooden kitchen table. Mark and Josh already knew. My father cracked his knuckles.

"I have a sister," he told me. "Her name is Edna."

I couldn't have been more shocked if he'd said he liked to dress up in women's lingerie and heels like those husbands on *Phil Donahue,* or if he'd announced we were moving to Alaska or Paris.

"We haven't spoken in a long time. My uncle Leo, my mother's older brother—your great-uncle—has gotten back in touch with me, and we've been talking on the phone. He's a sweet man, you'll like him."

My father had a brother, too. He was the real reason our phone number was unlisted, not because my mother was a teacher and might get prank calls, which was what my father always said when I'd asked why we couldn't be in the town phone book like everyone else.

The truth was, my father didn't speak to anyone in his family.

I was so stunned by my father's admission and so excited about this new batch of relatives that I didn't think to be angry with him for lying to me my entire life.

And there was more.

"We're going to go see Edna on Saturday," my father said. "She has two kids, they're older than you."

See them! That Saturday!

But we weren't going to see the brother, not ever. They didn't even tell me his name. My mother said he was bad news.

"That's why we always want you and Josh and Mark to be close," she explained. "All you have in this world is each other."

*　　*　　*

When Saturday morning came and it was time to meet our secret relatives, my mother had a migraine. I went up to her bedroom and stood in the doorway while she talked to my father from underneath the covers. The shades were drawn and the lights were off and the noise machine on her nightstand hissed. I turned around and went back down the stairs before they could notice me. A few minutes later he told us to get ready and said she wouldn't be coming with us. He didn't seem upset, even though he spent every second or third Sunday with his mother-in-law.

I wasn't surprised that she was staying home, either.

Conventional wisdom in our family held that my father was a near-genius who, though underpaid and generally unappreciated by the world at large, was tough and could handle almost anything. When my mother had a problem with her principal, he went in to help her negotiate. On Saturday mornings he'd spread the bills out on the kitchen table and work through them with his coffee and the calculator. He kept track of gas mileage with a notebook in the glove compartment. My mother had to balance her checkbook and show it to him; unlike her, he was an expert. Good with his hands, he spent the weekends fixing things around the house. Maybe he'd be repairing a car, or stripping and sanding the kitchen cabinets, or dealing with a plumbing leak under the kitchen sink, or tiling the downstairs bathroom. He always had something he was working on. She was more refined and middle-class; weaker, the family lore went, prone to illness and hypoglycemia and heart palpitations, at the mercy of hormone shifts and enduring exhaustion. Supposedly, she wasn't as smart as my father, who read the newspapers and listened to NPR when Imus wasn't on the radio. She read more books, though. And could beat him at Scrabble. He was better at strategy, but she knew more words.

On the car ride over, my brothers and I learned more about our father's childhood. Old stories were retold and reworked to make room for his having been not an only child after all, but the youngest of three. The egg salad sandwiches his mother packed for the beach that tasted crunchy with sand by lunchtime. Their apartment in Washington Heights getting so hot in the summer that on the warmest nights, my father strapped himself to the fire escape so he wouldn't fall off when he slept out there. Though his immigrant parents weren't particularly religious, they spoke Yiddish at home and sent my father to a yeshiva, a Jewish day school, where half the day was spent on Torah and Talmud and Hebrew studies. The lone nonobservant boy in school, he learned to take on one role in public and another in private. In the late afternoons he played stickball with the neighborhood boys until his mother called him in for dinner. They were poor, he said. His father worked at a corner grocery store.

And there was something else he wanted us to know.

"My father hit me," he said.

His declaration made me hold my breath.

"He'd use his belt or sometimes plumbing pipe. Anything he could get his hands on." My grandfather had wanted my grandmother to have a back-alley abortion since her later-in-life pregnancy—my father—was unwelcome, but she'd refused. Maybe that was why. "I was the one who found him when he died. He was on the toilet. He was having a heart attack. I was twelve. Part of me was relieved."

I had a hundred questions but couldn't ask any of them. Did my father want me to feel sorry for him? Was this his way of apologizing? Did this mean I was destined to hit my children, too?

He didn't come out and say this was why he hit us, but he didn't have to. I could tell, though, that he thought what he'd gone through had been worse, that plumbing pipe was harder and more unforgiving than hands, and that being

47

poor somehow made the violence count more. Which meant that maybe what happened in our house didn't really.

I stared out the window.

My father continued. Edna was his older sister. Unlike my parents and almost everyone else we knew, she hadn't gotten to go to college. When my father was a teenager, my grandmother had been in and out of psychiatric hospitals for depression or bipolar disorder, or possibly for schizophrenia, the details were murky. Edna had stayed in the family apartment and taken care of my father when my grandmother couldn't; he'd gone to a regular public high school after my grandfather died, then on to Columbia University with a full scholarship, but he wasn't able to compete with the prep school boys there. He struggled to get gentleman's C's. Their brother, the middle child, was psychologically unstable and jealous of my father for being the youngest and their mother's favorite and a college boy. These days he came and went and couldn't hold down a job and was always borrowing money. Sometimes Edna and my father would lock him out of the apartment. Once, when my father was in college, my uncle had shown up and pounded on the door, threatening to kill my father. They called the police on him.

*   *   *

We drove to somewhere in Brooklyn or Queens. My father said this was a working-class neighborhood with lots of Italians and Jews. Rockville Centre had Italians and

Jews, too, but this place didn't look anything like where we were from, even though we'd driven for less than an hour. The aluminum-sided row houses reminded me of *Archie Bunker's Place*. The streets were steaming and crowded and noisy with honking car horns and radios blaring from apartment windows. Older men in tank tops and women in housedresses sat on lawn chairs on the sidewalk, and children played in front of open fire hydrants, just like in a movie. My father told us to make sure the car doors were locked.

In my town, the kids with more money—some of whom I knew from Hebrew school—wore Jordache jeans and Champion sweatshirts and lived in big houses. Most but not all of the African-American kids ate school lunches and were "bused in" and came from "the projects," though I didn't really know what either of those things meant. My elementary school friends were mostly middle-class Irish or Italian Catholics and Jews. We seemed to have the normal, regular, *right* amount of money. Not enough for eight weeks of sleepaway camp but enough for a slice of Sicilian after school at Miceli's or Sal's or Palmeri's and a movie on the weekend. This was just the way things were.

My father found a spot and parallel-parked. Aunt Edna stepped out of the house and hurried to the car to greet us. She was wearing a flowered muumuu and had a perm and a thick New York accent. By comparison, my father's (still-strong) accent seemed all-American, like a newscaster's. She hugged my brothers and me, a warm and tight embrace, like she was really, truly happy to see us, before leading

49

the way to the front door and into the kitchen to meet our cousins. Edna's daughter was in her early twenties, and her son was a teenager. If I'm remembering right, they both lived at home. The daughter had bright pastel eye makeup and a much older non-Jewish, divorced Italian-American fiancé with kids from his previous relationship and tattoos on his biceps. (My mother had told me and my brothers many times that she'd sit *shiva* for us and pretend we were dead if we married a non-Jew or got tattoos, which she said would mean we couldn't be buried in a Jewish cemetery.)

My father shook his brother-in-law's hand. "It's been a long time," he said.

"Too long," said my newfound uncle.

"Sit, sit," Edna said. "I have food. We're going to grill. Martin, would you like some coffee? Or a beer?"

In the kitchen, the question of their brother came up.

"He calls," Edna said, shrugging. "Sometimes he comes by and eats through the whole refrigerator. Then I won't hear from him for a while. Not for months, even."

"I want nothing to do with him," my father said. "Whatever you do, don't give him my number. Make sure he doesn't get in touch with me." Edna looked disappointed but resigned and nodded her agreement. My father had stopped talking to her sometime after their mother died. It had been over ten years. It was enough for her to have us in her house. She wouldn't push.

I played with an electric train set in the basement with my new uncle and the younger of my two cousins. My brothers played catch with a baseball in the yard, but they seemed uncomfortable. I decided I wouldn't be. I liked Edna and her family. They were nicer and more fun than my grandmother, even though they wore too much polyester.

Edna telephoned a few days later. My older cousin and her fiancé wanted to invite me to Six Flags Great Adventure, just me without my brothers. My parents had what they called a "heated discussion" because my mother didn't think this was a good idea. My father said it would be fine. I was to sleep over at Aunt Edna's the night before so we could leave for the New Jersey amusement park first thing. I wanted to go, sort of, but when my father dropped me off, I realized I was in a house full of stranger-relatives, and I felt way too young to be navigating the situation by myself. I wasn't sure why my parents had let me come after all.

The following morning the park was hot, and I got a headache from the sun and the roller coasters and the candy, but my cousin and her boyfriend were good to me, buying me trinkets and letting me go on as many rides as I wanted. Still, I knew my mother looked down on this family though she was trying her best to accept them for my father's sake. She called them *low class* when she thought I couldn't hear.

* * *

Not long after, we went to see our great-uncle, my paternal grandmother Ruth's brother. Ruth had come to New York before the war, but her brother, Leo, had stayed behind in

Europe. A family of Polish farmers hid Leo in their barn during the Holocaust. My father called them righteous gentiles. Great-aunt Bertha, whom Leo married soon after the war, had been sent to Auschwitz, where she was, my father explained, "experimented on" by the Nazis. Because of those forced surgeries and other unimaginable abuses, Bertha suffered from psychiatric and medical issues for the rest of her life, and she and Leo weren't able to have children. By the time we came to know them, they must have been in their sixties, though they seemed older. Bertha lived in a nursing home, where Leo faithfully visited her every day. Years before, arriving in New York, Leo had opened a small grocery, then another. My grandfather and the other brothers, whom I'd never meet, worked with (or was it for?) him. My father said there was some tension between the brothers about their business dealings. Leo was the successful one, the envied brother, but he lived simply, preferring to send money every month to the Polish family who had saved him, eventually helping some of them immigrate to America.

It was Leo who'd originally contacted my father and was trying to piece the family back together. We drove to Manhattan to see him. Once again, my brothers and I came along and my mother stayed home.

Leo lived in a large, mostly empty apartment deep on the Lower East Side. My father said that it was rent-controlled and taught me what that meant. I'd never heard the word *rent* before, though when I played with my friends, we liked to pretend we were models or dancers or actresses living in

New York City. This wasn't that New York. We walked up a dark and dank staircase and down a long hallway.

"Come in, come in," Leo said, opening the heavy door wide. "My darlinks! You are here."

Leo was an old, skinny, dear man with hollow cheeks and a worn suit jacket and trousers. There was poetry in his humble manner and not a hint of big-city glamour. The way he wore a newsboy cap and tucked a cigarette in the crook of his ear moved me. He smelled like cigarettes, in the best way, and of sour pickles and smoked fish. He had stacks of newspapers around, and was playing music on the radio when we came in. His fingers were yellow with tobacco stains, and he put his hands out to cradle my face and stare into my eyes. I loved him from the first moment.

That February, or perhaps the one after, Leo came to Josh's bar mitzvah. Edna's family was invited, too. (My mother wasn't thrilled about that, but what could she do?) Mark's bar mitzvah celebration two years earlier had been a small reception at home after services with an accordion player and catering and rented tables. For Josh, who had more friends and cared about these things and begged to have a "normal" party, my parents threw a big reception at a country club with a DJ and photographer. My mother seated my father's relatives at a table in the back, far from her teacher friends.

After the family reunion, Edna called my father every week and then every couple of weeks. He didn't call her, and then, after a while, he stopped returning her calls. She moved to Texas with her family a few years later. We never saw Edna or our cousins again.

We kept in touch with Leo, though. One early fall day a year or two later, my father and I were supposed to go see him. We hadn't been in a while, but this visit had been planned for a long time. That morning the girl who lived across the street from us called and asked if I wanted to walk into town. We'd hang out in the summer and catch fireflies or rehearse our next talent show or dance in her bedroom to "Don't You Want Me" by the Human League, but she hardly ever asked me to do anything during the school year, much less take the very public walk into town, because she was one of the popular girls and I wasn't. I covered the receiver with my shirt and asked my father what to do.

"Go with your friend," he said. He knew I struggled with fitting in at school. But I hesitated, thinking about Leo alone in his apartment.

"No, that's okay," I decided, saying goodbye to her and hanging up the phone. I wasn't trying to be a saint, but I knew it was the right thing to do. Besides, I missed Leo. We drove in and sat in his bare rooms and cracked walnuts. Leo let me interview him for an oral history report for Hebrew school, using a cloth handkerchief to wipe away the tears that fell down his face like cigarette ash as he talked about his past. Then we went over to visit Bertha. We met her in the recreation room. She was using a wheelchair and smelled like hospitals, like the way the inside of my mouth tasted when I needed a drink of water. I sat next to her until my father made me stand up in front of the room and sing. I chose "My Favorite Things" but worried over the *crisp apple strudel* and *schnitzel with noodles* lines, wondering if that

54

brought back bad memories. After that I sang the theme song from the movie *Fame*: *I'm gonna live forever / I'm gonna learn how to fly / High!* I ended with "Matchmaker" from *Fiddler on the Roof* because I figured the Jewish residents would like that one.

FOUR

BEING JEWISH MATTERED to my parents, and it mattered
to my brothers and me, too. Israel, the Holocaust, and Hebrew school were our holy trinity. When we'd moved to
Rockville Centre and it had come time to pick a temple, my
parents had gone back and forth between the Reform and
Conservative synagogues in town, weighing the theological
pros and cons. At Central Synagogue, the Reform temple
a few blocks from our house, women read from the Torah,
and some of them even wore *kippot,* yarmulkes, pinned
onto their wavy hair and *tallit,* prayer shawls, around their
shoulders. I liked Central because the mothers in the congregation seemed thoughtful and laid-back in their loose
skirts and clogs, because the sermons were more peaceful
and hopeful-sounding, and because the older boys were
cuter and some of them paired their High Holiday rumpled
shirts and ties with Converse sneakers. Much of the service
was in English, though, and the Hebrew songs and prayer
melodies were different from what my parents, especially
my father, were used to hearing. He and my mother said
they felt like they were in church.

My mother hadn't been brought up especially observant and didn't know how to read Hebrew. Like many Jewish women of her generation, she hadn't had a bat mitzvah or much of a Jewish education. But she gravitated to the moral absolutes that religion can provide, and she felt flattered that we were the chosen people. We weren't kosher and didn't keep Shabbat, but we celebrated the High Holy Days and Hanukkah, and observed Passover with two seders at home and no bread or pasta for a week, and we went to the annual Purim carnival put on by my Hebrew school. When we ate out at Ben's Kosher Delicatessen, my mother knew enough to be embarrassed when Josh tried to order a cheeseburger. The important thing, she said, was having Jewish children and making sure they married Jews. She told me she had three because the rabbis said it was necessary to replace yourself and your husband and then add an extra Jew for those who'd been killed during the Holocaust.

B'nai Shalom, the Conservative synagogue that my parents decided to join, was a totally different scene from Central. Women wore panty hose and pumps and expensive outfits and had their hair done, and some had furs. Girls wore frilly dresses and shiny patent-leather shoes. Men and boys wore dark suits and dress shoes. Women of the congregation could come up to the bimah, the synagogue podium, for readings or to make announcements, but they weren't allowed to read from the Torah—though girls could for one day only, on their bat mitzvah. I figured we weren't considered one hundred percent equal before the eyes of God or even the eyes of the rabbi. For one thing, women didn't count toward the minyan, the daily prayer quorum made up of Kaddish-reciting mourners and a few devout everyday religious men who met in the small auxiliary chapel.

The High Holidays meant new outfits, and expensive admission tickets to raise funds for the synagogue, and sermons about Israel or Russian Refuseniks and marathon day-into-evening services with overflow crowds. I liked that my father wore a *tallis*. During the long, drawn-out services, I'd lean my head in the crook of his arm and braid the strings dangling from the cloth. With the prayer book open between us, he'd move his index finger from right to left underneath the Hebrew words so that I could follow along. When I got bored, I'd escape to the women's lounge and fish old cigarettes out of the ashtrays, holding the red-lipstick-stained butts to my mouth in front of the gilded vanity mirrors while nobody was looking.

I went to Hebrew school on Sunday mornings and two days after school. We studied Hebrew, prayer and Torah, Jewish history, and biblical interpretation. We committed to memory prayers like Ma Tovu and Adon Olam and the Ashrei and learned to read (but not understand) enough Hebrew to hopefully one day get through our bar and bat mitzvahs. When our teachers were overwhelmed or absent, we'd watch *Raid on Entebbe* or *Hester Street,* the teacher covering the screen with her hands during the sex scene.

The best part of Hebrew school, as far as I was concerned, was library time. Once a week we lined up and walked down the hall from the classrooms, being shushed by our teacher the whole way and warned not to disturb the other classes, though there was no quieting us. The same children who were teachers' pets in regular public school turned rowdy and arrogantly dismissive here. In class we ignored the lectures on Talmudic teachings while boys tipped back their chairs, cracked jokes, and snapped the bras of the few girls who needed them, making fun of the rest of us. But when we entered the corner library, a miraculous hush fell over the room. This was the one truly holy place in the entire school. We settled quietly on the carpeted floor and took our spots by the feet of Mrs. Avner, the librarian. She perched her petite frame on a stool and read from classic Jewish children's literature like *The Adventures of K'Ton Ton* and Isaac Bashevis Singer's *Stories for Children* when we were little, and now that we were older, the *All-of-a-Kind Family* series about the adventures of five sisters growing up with poor but loving immigrant parents on the Lower East Side. We closed our eyes and traveled with her to faraway places. Israel, Europe, New York City.

After she was done reading, we had a few minutes to browse the small but expertly curated collection and make our selections before heading to the parking lot and waiting for our rides home. We could check out two books each. Combing the familiar shelves, I accumulated a fast and greedy pile of maybes, and made sure to ask Mrs. Avner for help deciding. She'd steer me toward more challenging titles or a guilty pleasure I wouldn't have found myself. One day she let me and another devoted reader named Stefanie—a girl I'd hoped to befriend since the second grade—stay after the other kids had left, and gave us permission to take a whole stack home over a school vacation.

Over the years Mrs. Avner handed me, among other titles, *Summer of My German Soldier,* which blended Holocaust YA lit with a thrillingly steamy interfaith romance, and Anne Frank's *Diary* and then *Night* by Elie Wiesel. I devoured them and came back asking for more. Maybe it was because bad things were happening to me at home that I was drawn to Holocaust literature, stories of events and a time unimaginably, immeasurably, worse than Long Island circa 1984. Maybe it was because of Leo and Bertha; maybe it was just what Jewish girls do. But, above all other subjects, I read obsessively about the Warsaw Ghetto and Bergen-Belsen and Auschwitz and the train rides to the concentration camps, and about children being separated from their parents at the gates, and about the death walk to the gas chambers.

My father was late to pick me up one evening, and I stood shivering and hungry in the darkening parking lot with my two new books in my hand and my regular school things, Trapper Keepers and hardcover textbooks and spiral subject notebooks, weighing down my backpack.

Was there a God? It was a question I thought about a lot, especially when I was at B'nai. Most days I believed there was, because when I sat next to my father in services braiding his prayer shawl, I felt something well up in my chest—a presence, an energy, a sort of comforting hand on my forehead. When I studied the stained-glass synagogue windows, and sometimes when I lay in my bed at night and prayed, I imagined there was someone on the other end of those prayers. But the rest of the time I felt completely, horribly, terribly alone. When my father hit me or yelled. When my parents fought. And what about the Holocaust and the photographs we'd been shown of the dead children's shoes? What of Anne Frank? What about Leo and Bertha? And the children starving in Africa? What about my mother sitting on the toilet crying, with wads of toilet paper in her hands?

"Sorry," my father said, pulling up next to me in the lot and reaching over to unlock the passenger door. I was usually one of the last kids to be picked up, but he was almost twenty minutes late, which was unusual. I didn't like having to wait for him in the cold. "Traffic."

"That's okay," I said, settling into the passenger seat and changing the radio station. "Do you believe in God?" I asked, throwing my backpack and books on the seat behind me.

"No," he said, sighing and turning out of the parking lot. "Not really. But there's no way to be a hundred percent sure. That's why I'm more of an agnostic than an atheist."

"I know what that means. We talked about it in Hebrew school. Being an atheist means you definitely don't believe in God, and agnostic means you can't decide," I said.

"There probably isn't, though," he answered.

I looked out the window and drew two intersecting triangles on the thin layer of frost and breath, one upside down and the other right side up, a tiny Star of David.

"But there might be," I said, because that should be the last thing in the conversation, just in case God was listening.

Mrs. Avner eventually left our small suburban synagogue library, taking a position as a children's librarian at the 92nd Street Y in Manhattan. When she said goodbye, she promised we'd stay in touch, but I was surprised a few months later when she invited me to the Y for the day. One morning she picked me up in her car and we drove to the Upper East Side. She gave me a tour of the grand-seeming building and library, and I sat in on story hour with the younger children. At lunchtime, we went out for kosher Chinese food. Walking briskly and purposefully through the city streets, as it seemed everyone did in Manhattan, was the very best part. I was floored by Mrs. Avner's cosmopolitan, intellectual career and by her knowledge of books. I sat on the banquette, sipping my wonton soup, working my chopsticks over chicken and broccoli, and thinking, *Why can't my mother be more like this?* I so wanted to tell Mrs. Avner about my father.

* * *

When Mark was in eleventh grade, he regenerated worms for a science fair project, cutting them in two and observing them as they grew back. He taught the intact worms a behavior, using food for a reward and a shock for punishment, and then halved them to see if their new selves remembered their training after the severing. He started the experiment in science class but kept the worms at home in his bedroom before taking them to the Westinghouse Science Talent Search semifinals. I remember being struck by the cruelty of the project, yet fascinated by the idea that we could be sliced in two and somehow come back new and different and whole, retaining something of our old selves. My brothers seemed like those worms to me. They appeared indestructible and resilient, not easily wrecked by the harm inflicted by our father, where I was vulnerable and easily harmed. When I was sliced, I split and became broken.

By then Mark and Josh were too old for me. They were never home. Or they were home but all of their friends were over. I would go into my brothers' room and listen to their records by myself, but it wasn't the same. They were two years apart but had different roles in the family. Josh was exuberant and fun-loving, always after a good time, and surrounded by a loyal crew of friends. Mark, like my father, was supposed to be the smart one. He seemed to have everything going for him. He earned top grades and was nice-looking, too, with dark hair and eyes. On top of being a Boy Scout, Mark was on the newspaper and yearbook.

Plus, he had a head for business. We called him Richie Rich, after the boy-millionaire cartoon character, and later, Alex P. Keaton, when the sitcom *Family Ties* came on. My parents trusted Mark to be in charge of Josh and me when they weren't home, and my father confided in him about the family finances and his work problems. My parents pinned their hopes on him like one of his Boy Scout merit badges. Mark would be the one to be successful. He was the child they didn't have to worry about. They looked to him for advice even when he was in high school. They joked that he would take care of them financially when they were older, but you could tell they weren't necessarily kidding.

My parents were in their early forties, stressed about bills and college prices and retirement funds. After the gas lines and the hostage crisis and the sweater-wearing Carter years, they'd split their vote (I think) between Carter and Reagan in 1980, my mother sticking with the Democrats. Now, four years later, it was "morning in America," according to the political commercial that gave me goose bumps, although I despised Reagan. Like the rest of the country, my parents were growing less liberal on social issues and more conservative on the economy and foreign policy. They both voted for Reagan's reelection that fall.

My brothers announced that they were Republicans, too. They wanted pastel Polo shirts and Sony Walkmans and stereos and sushi dinners and foreign exchange trips to the Soviet Union and Spain, and one day their own cars, and they were willing to work for them. What mattered, Josh and Mark decided, was to make money. Money equaled freedom.

But Mark worried about not having "connections" when it came to the real world, and he complained that our parents couldn't help him land an eventual job or even a summer internship because they were middle-class suburbanites with no ties to Manhattan elites.

Josh didn't care about a fancy degree or job the way Mark did. He wanted to make money, too, but he liked Long Island and wasn't in a hurry to leave. Josh could be fun to hang out with, when he wasn't teasing or ignoring me, but I was in awe of Mark, who was old enough to seem impossibly mature. We all knew Mark was going places. He would become the success our father should have been.

Despite how tough that must have been on Josh, my brothers were best friends. Mark got better grades, yes, but Josh was more likable and popular, and that helped even things out. They hosted Ping-Pong tournaments in our garage and eight-ball pool games in our basement and summer pool parties in our backyard. They started busing tables at a Japanese restaurant in town called Taiko and sometimes worked winter weekends at Taiko's sushi bar on a ski mountain. They drank beer (mostly Josh), and worked hard in school (mostly Mark), and played sports. The pure boy smell of their room was made up of dirty white tube socks and an overflowing laundry hamper. Change jars sat on top of dressers, team uniforms were slung over desk chairs, backpacks jammed with homework and textbooks lay on the floor, and *Penthouse* magazines were buried deep underneath their beds.

Because I was the only girl, and the youngest, I felt left out. I objected to being grouped with my mother, whom Mark loved but thought prissy and straight-laced and lacking self-control about her weight and not intellectual enough. He and our father and Josh had all the good times.

But Mark and I were close, too, and emotionally tied

in our own way. I was no boy genius or wunderkind like him, but I got good grades, and he saw me as (almost) his intellectual equal. What really separated us from the rest of the family, though, was our shared desire to get out of Rockville Centre. Mark made me feel that, in this way, I was like him. We were potential sophisticates stuck in the wrong town, but not for long. Together, Mark and I were haughty and unabashedly judgmental about our surroundings, the homecoming floats and football games. We felt we were different, and we wanted more than what we saw around us. We would never raise our kids in a place like Rockville Centre. We would travel and see the world.

What I remember most about Mark is the way he would protect me, the way that, when I needed him, he was there for me. He could make me feel safe, which was all I ever really wanted. We'd cuddle in bed together. I remember how his comforter was blue on one side and red on the other. I loved how warm he was, how good he smelled.

* * *

My father had started his career working for the New York City Department of Education straight out of college. His first job was as a math teacher at Canarsie High School in Brooklyn. We had a photo of him in the classroom, young, skinny, and bright-eyed, with a short-sleeve white button-down shirt and black Buddy Holly glasses, posing and smiling between desks of students who looked almost his age. He told us stories about being a rookie teacher, just a couple of years older than his students because he had skipped a grade. There was a funny one about the time he split his pants during class. And another about when he asked his students how many of them had been to Manhattan, which was a straight shot on the L train. Only one or two raised their hands. This was a sad story, because it meant they didn't take advantage of the city like we did, driving in a few times a year for museums or Yankees games or a Broadway show or Chinatown dim sum.

He'd gone on to study for a Ph.D. in educational psychology at Hofstra, finishing his dissertation, "The Effects of Time of Informative Feedback and Type of Interpolated Learning on the Retention of Meaningful, Connected, Verbal Material," in 1975, when I was three. He'd been a researcher at LaGuardia Community College for as long as I could remember.

But one day I started hearing grumblings around our house. Phone calls and hushed, worried conversations between my parents. My father was in danger of losing his job. I tried to eavesdrop and figure out exactly what was going on. It sounded like my father and some others in his office had been accused of falsifying research results. I thought I overheard something about playing around with the numbers. The whole thing was bullshit, according to my father. He said the college had *asked him* to manipulate the research data to prove their programs were successful. But we weren't supposed to know or talk about any of it.

I didn't know what to believe. I was embarrassed, worried, and scared about my father losing his job, and of course

I was ashamed, but I wasn't surprised or shocked. I was used to the little lies and cheats and ways to steal things and save money where we could. When people in the neighborhood started getting cable, my father wanted to watch the fights on HBO but not pay for them. One Saturday he put my brothers on lookout while he climbed up a telephone pole behind our yard and did some fiddling. Bingo! We had cable. A few years later Josh brought home a descrambling device he'd bought from a guy who knew a guy. My mother didn't like it, but my father said it was staying. Why should we give our money to Cablevision? That kind of stealing didn't count. We needed the money, and those companies had enough already. We got every channel, including late-night porn that my brothers would sometimes sneak, all for free. I was guilty, too. With my father's blessing, my brothers signed up for those eleven-cassette-tapes-for-a-penny music clubs using fake names, and they taught me to do the same. When we eventually made it to Disney World, my father made me pretend to be under twelve to get the discount. At Friendly's, where we went for my favorite chicken-tender dinners, he had me lie about my age to get the children's meal. *The system is working*, my father and brothers would joke whenever we got away with something.

Those were small lies, though. So small they hardly counted. Everyone stole cable, my father said. Besides, he had never gotten caught before, not that I knew about. This time was different; this time was serious. My father was fired from the college. (We weren't supposed to say *fired*, we were supposed to say *let go*.) It could have been worse. A severance package was offered. A small buyout. He'd get to collect his pension. But he was out of a job and a career, too. He would never go back on the academic job market. As an excuse to her teacher friends, my mother murmured something about budget cuts. But as far as I was concerned, my father was a cheater, and because of it, our world was about to end. Without his salary, we couldn't pay the mortgage, much less college for Mark and then Josh two years later.

Frantic, my father called his old math department chair, Len, who had long ago stopped teaching and owned a direct-mail magazine subscription service specializing in selling discounted subscriptions to doctors and dentists and teachers' associations. Len said that my father should run a small business. This sounded about right to my father. Your own business meant freedom, he explained to my mother. He wanted to be his own boss. He met with a business broker who helped people buy and sell small businesses like a real estate agent sells houses or apartments. I went with my parents to look at a storefront candy and news-paper store in a nearby town, similar to what his father and uncles once owned.

It was too much of a risk, my mother thought. The hours! And what would we do when it didn't work out? We had a mortgage and bills to pay and three kids to send to college.

Instead, my father tried out the idea of becoming a busi-ness broker himself. He'd work on commission. That lasted a few more months, while my mother's panic increased on a daily basis. Mark was worried sick, too. You couldn't count on commissions. How were they going to afford tuition? Even with loans and financial aid, parents were expected to make a sizable contribution. Things got worse around the house. There were raised arms and voices and slammed doors, except when my father made a sale, and then, like gamblers after a big win, we celebrated. And for a few weeks everything was okay. But when a sale fell through, we were the ones who paid.

Eventually my father persuaded Len to give him a job at the subscription firm. His Ph.D. looked good in the signature of sales letters. He could go to trade association meetings and schmooze like he was one of them. Nobody would need to know the truth about why he'd left academia.

*　　*　　*

Late spring. Time to weed the front and side yards and trim back the bushes. My brothers and I were supposed to help our father with this job, but I didn't like the sight of him with a hedge trimmer in his hands.

I was supposed to follow him around and fill the yard trash can with cuttings. My brothers always had the more difficult chores, vacuuming the pool or weeding or raking leaves or shoveling snow, but I had to do my share, too. After a few minutes I started sneezing and couldn't stop because of my allergies. My father scowled at me.

That was pretty fucking convenient for me, wasn't it? I was always trying to take the easy way out, wasn't I?

When my mother came outside, he told her I was trying to get out of my chores again.

This time, I remember distinctly, she tried to reason with him. "She's allergic to the grass and pollen."

"She's a little spoiled brat, is what she is. There's always an excuse when it comes time to work."

I kept sneezing. I sneezed five and six times in a row. I wasn't making up the sneezes, but I made a show of them. Sometimes I rebelled by pushing back against the fear, by pushing back against him. I couldn't help my allergies, could I?

He told me to go into the kitchen to take some Dimetapp. I returned to my post by the bushes with a wad of tissues and complaints about the heat. I had a headache, I felt like throwing up.

He took off his yard gloves and turned off the hedge trimmer but held on to it while he let me have it. *Ungrateful.* I was a priss, just like my mother, he muttered half to himself and half to me. He had to be careful because we were outside, where the neighbors could hear. It was safer in the front yard, but I ran into the house to get away from him anyway. Fuck him.

I ran up the stairs. I was sick of being terrified of my father and how much he might hurt me. I didn't care anymore if he hit me. Let him. My daily vigilance had exhausted me. Nobody loved me, I told myself. I was certain nobody ever would.

* * *

Josh and Mark's Scout troop met in the basement of Central Synagogue, where they hoisted the American flag before every meeting, wearing their olive green and tan uniforms, sashes festooned with merit badges. Once every year or two they went on a wilderness adventure trip, usually camping in eastern Canada or canoeing or tubing upstate. Both my brothers were serious about scouting, especially Mark. By the time he was seventeen, he was a couple of badges away from becoming an Eagle Scout. Eagle Scout was a big deal. It could help you get into college and get scholarships, and it meant you were an upstanding and moral citizen, a model young man. There'd even be an article about you in the Rockville Centre *News and Owl*. You could get the most merit badges in the shortest amount of time at Boy Scout camp, and every summer my brothers would drive up with their scoutmaster and some other boys from their troop. They swam across the lake and practiced survival skills and lifesaving and tying rope into knots and archery and whatever else went on in the woods. It wasn't unusual for a father to join the troop as a chaperone and sort of senior counselor. They needed volunteers. One summer when my brothers were in high school and I was in middle school, our father signed up. They'd all three be gone for two whole weeks in August.

Two weeks! I wanted those weeks to last forever. All summer long, I lay in bed in the mornings, fantasizing about taking care of my mother and showing her how good I could be. I counted down the days until we'd be alone. I wanted to prove how nice things would be if she would gather the strength to leave him, even if it did mean selling the house and moving to an apartment, an idea that was sounding better and better to me. I'd bike all the way to Brower Avenue for bagels and make her breakfast. She would play with my hair and I would rub her feet. We would read at the table. I would bring her flowers.

When my father and brothers took their army-navy-store duffel bags and backpacks and pulled out of the driveway, my mother sat in the kitchen and called her friend Madeline to make a date for shopping and lunch. Then she brought her magazines and novel to the chaise lounge in the backyard. We had two wood patio deck chairs that reclined at three different positions. The yellow cushions were waterproof, but my father made sure to bring them into the garage every night, so they'd stay nice longer. With him gone, there'd be a chair for each of us. But my mother wasn't thinking about me. She was exhausted. *Did I know how hard she worked?* She deserved this time to herself with an almost empty house. She shooed me away.

I was crushed. On an afternoon walk with a friend, I brought home a sad bunch of yellow daisies from a vacant lot, but my mother was allergic and had to leave them on the back stoop, and the next morning, when I threw out Snoopy's poop after taking him for a walk, I found them in the garbage.

A few days later, without warning, my father and brothers came home early. Josh and Mark looked sweaty and dirty and sunburned and spent, but not in the normal just back from sleeping in the woods tired and satisfied and ready for a good night's sleep and a hot meal kind of way. It seemed like they were hiding something. My father was pissed off. They dropped their bags in the laundry room and went upstairs to shower. Nobody explained why they were home unexpectedly. Nobody said anything. I wouldn't find out until years later, when I went to a diner with my brothers to try and talk to them about the abuse. Mark confessed to me that my father had been kicked out of Boy Scout camp for hitting Josh and another camper.

*   *   *

His senior year of high school, Mark started going jogging, which meant he was sneaking out to have sex with his secret non-Jewish girlfriend who lived a few blocks away. She was blond and pretty and got good grades, and I was jealous of her. My mother didn't want to know anything about it. He wasn't allowed to take her to the prom or even bring her over. Mark let this injustice go. He was busy applying to colleges and determined to get into the University of Pennsylvania, where he hoped to major in business at Wharton. He and my father had argued about the amount to fill in on the financial aid forms under suggested parental contribution. My father wrote in five thousand dollars. Which Mark said was a joke, and the reason he didn't get accepted early decision. But Mark would end up with a full-ride academic scholarship to the undergraduate business program at Washington University in St. Louis.

Jessica Berger Gross

With Mark gone, I gave up on the idea of being rescued. Instead, I started biking around my neighborhood in the late afternoons and on weekends, trying to get lost. I'd ride along the familiar streets, zooming left and then right and then left again, until I confused myself and didn't know how to find my way back home.

FIVE

BY EIGHTH GRADE, I spent most of my time at home by myself. It was a relief. My parents stayed downstairs, and I stayed in my room. Josh was in eleventh grade and avoiding our parents, who were on his case about grades and SAT prep. When he was home, his friends were usually over. They'd rent movies from the video store or play poker or pool, and I would hang around the family room or basement until Josh kicked me out. Sometimes I'd call Mark at college and talk to him with the door closed, but there was only so much I could say. Not being able to confide in anyone about the truth of my home life, I started a diary. One middle school entry: *My dad's such a jerk. He blew up at me. He didn't hit me, but he called me bitch and every other curse word. Dad's a dick. What else can I say about it?*

But I was afraid of what would happen when my mother found my diary and read it. (She didn't hesitate to search my brothers' room for contraband.) I soon quit writing down what was happening, and instead, hidden away in my bedroom, I'd escape by cheating on my diet and eating pistachios and rereading my favorite paperbacks. I devoured *Seventeenth Summer,* the 1942 novel chronicling a chaste summer romance in Wisconsin; and *Flowers in the Attic,* about an abused and incestuous brother-sister couple; and a retro girlie romance-laden take on the *Choose Your Own Adventure* books; and *Sunshine* by Norma Klein, a love story about a young mother dying of cancer; and *I Know Why the Caged Bird Sings* by Maya Angelou.

In Ascent, our school's gifted program, I lip-synced to Madonna and wrote and directed a soap opera–style short featuring my drama club classmates. (My new friend Kathy and I were loyal viewers of *Santa Barbara,* starring Robin Wright.) For a book report in language arts, I decided to do my project on *Sybil,* a book I'd borrowed from my mother that told the supposedly true story of a sexually, physically, and emotionally abused girl who grows up to suffer from multiple personality disorder. Reading in bed with my feet tucked inside a blanket, I devoured the abuse scenes. What Sybil went through was far worse, I assured myself, than what happened to me, yet I found myself relating. On the other hand, since her abuse was so much more serious, maybe mine didn't count. Sybil's mother had tied her up and given her forced enemas and stuck fingers inside her. All my father did was yell and hit. All my mother did was stay.

The assignment was to construct a diorama depicting an important moment from the book we'd read. Using my mother's old shoe box that once housed her good black leather boots, I spent a weekend on the floor of my room, reconstructing one of the sexual abuse scenes. I wasn't very crafty, and perhaps the teacher didn't get what I was going for, but in my mind, at least, I tried to stay faithful to the book: Sybil, symbolized by a Little People figure, hanged by a lightbulb cord from the ceiling while her mother, a smiling yellow-haired Barbie doll, pointed a kitchen knife in the direction of her vagina.

Our dioramas were displayed in the classroom for weeks. My classmates looked at me funny when they saw mine. I got an A+.

When I wasn't reading, I watched too much TV. I watched *The Best Little Girl in the World* and wished I could have the discipline to become anorexic and weigh under 100 pounds so I could go live in a nice hospital. I watched *The Day After* and fantasized about a nuclear holocaust putting an end to my problems. I wished my parents would break up, like the parents in *Kramer vs. Kramer*. Or else I wanted to divorce my parents, like Drew Barrymore did in *Irreconcilable Differences*.

When *Mommie Dearest* was first shown on broadcast television, I somehow got away with staying up to watch it. Kitschy as it might seem looking back, Faye Dunaway as the actress Joan Crawford screaming, "No more wire hangers!" at her daughter, Christina, was by far the closest, most realistic depiction of my home life I'd ever encountered. This was pretty much what was happening to me. I recognized it all: the occasional, unpredictable violence and name-calling, the hurling of everyday objects, and the importance placed on keeping up appearances. For years I watched that movie every time it came on. Once or twice on a weekend afternoon my father came in the room and watched with me for a few minutes, not saying much.

*   *   *

On Saturdays, I'd stay in bed late sleeping lightly, half-awake-daydreaming or worrying or listening to the chords of conversation—arguments, usually—rising from the kitchen.

I couldn't be sure if the fighting was the kind to worry about. Sometimes, now that we were older, it was my father and Josh (or Mark, when he was home from college) having an odd kind of loud and argumentative "fun." Sometimes it was my parents needling each other or kibitzing, as my father called it. But the line between joking around and getting my father angry for real was thin. Even these morning squabbles could easily become something more. I'd stay in my bed as long as I could hold my pee, trying to figure out when it was safe to come out.

"Do you want to go shopping?" my mother asked me one morning when I eventually came downstairs.

My mother usually went clothes shopping on the weekends but hadn't left the house yet. Going along with her was a double-edged sword. If I went, then I'd have to *be* with her, to suffer through the awkward silences and try and fight off the barrage of supposedly constructive criticism. *Jessie, brush your hair. Jessie, is that what you're wearing? Jessie, why do you have to always look so messy?* I tried to ignore her, not to let her judgments and criticisms penetrate me. Brushing my hair, I knew, would make it frizzier. Nothing was wrong with what I was wearing, I told myself. Nothing was wrong with me. It was important to stand up to my mother, but I didn't know how.

On the upside, there would be new clothes. Like my mother, I loved clothes and craved the rush of something new. I pored over the *Seventeen* fashion spreads and studied how my favorite television characters dressed, like Denise Huxtable from *The Cosby Show*. My mother wanted me to look preppy and classy. I wanted to pull together a quirky vintage style, like Molly Ringwald in a John Hughes movie.

I opened the door of our yellow fridge. My father's chocolate Entenmann's donuts were waiting for me on the middle shelf, as were tubs of Philadelphia cream cheese to go with the bag of bagels we had on the counter. I knew I'd find a box of Cheerios in the pantry, which I could have with milk and a banana, but I'd always pour more milk than necessary, just to be safe, and then, when I was out of Cheerios but still had milk left, I'd pour a second bowl, which left me with too much cereal for the remaining milk. Which meant I'd have to add more milk, and then somehow my virtuous breakfast would end up a three-bowl special. Even breakfast was complicated.

I had to be careful, because I was thin, or at least on my way to thin, for the first time I could remember. My eighth-grade English teacher asked us to write a letter to our twelfth-grade selves and promised she'd mail the notes to us before our high school graduation. My three wishes to myself: *1) Lose weight*; *2) Get the lead in the high school plays*; *3) Have a boyfriend.* To my mind, numbers two and three depended entirely on number one. And so I decided to take matters into my own hands and set out on a path of self-improvement. Every night before I went to sleep, I devoted myself to reading my new bible, *The Sweet Dreams Body Book.* In keeping with the author's plan, I'd been eating sensibly, exercising my heart out, and watching my calories. Instead of unlimited bagels, I allowed myself unlimited baby carrots. My mother bought me an air popper to make fresh popcorn and started keeping more than one kind of fruit in the house. I tried my first green pepper and an unripe, cold supermarket tomato. I ate open-faced sandwiches and baked potatoes without butter and raw broccoli. I sucked on lemons and ice cubes to quiet my always needy appetite. When my motivation wavered, I would lie in bed and visualize myself in a bathing suit. I went for exercise walks, did pliés in the kitchen, and executed Jane Fonda–style leg lifts and sit-ups in front of the television before dinner. I danced in my room and went for jogs. It worked. My jeans were looser each week. When I stretched out in bed and rested my hands on my chest, I could even feel my ribs.

"Jessie? Do you want to come or don't you? Make up your mind, because I'm leaving soon. Bloomingdale's is having a sale," my mother said, showing me the glossy white postcard announcing the preseason sale for this weekend only. She generally had us hunt for brand-name bargains at discount emporiums. But during a big sale, or when she needed to return something or treat herself, or if we were shopping for a special occasion, she'd take me to Garden

City. My mother had a sweep of department store credit cards for Lord & Taylor and Saks and Macy's filling up the slots in her wallet, but Bloomingdale's was my favorite. I couldn't help but say yes. Garden City!

I went upstairs and got ready to go, brushing my teeth at the sink, putting my head under the faucet to rinse before spitting out my Aquafresh. My mother was usually tired, but she almost always found the energy to take me shopping. That was pretty much the point of having a daughter.

"Jessie!" my mother called from the kitchen, where I knew she'd be waiting with her arms folded against her chest and her keys in her hand.

It was hard to fill up the silences of the twenty-minute car ride to Garden City. I wasn't even sure my mother liked me. I figured she wanted me to be the kind of girl who was asked out on dates and to school dances so we could plan my outfit and then, the next morning, dissect the evening over breakfast. But I'd never held a boy's hand, or gotten a phone call from one, or been invited to a boy-girl house party.

I looked out the window and settled into my seat, soothed by the familiar click of my mother's turn signal. Her biggest concern for me was her biggest concern for herself, too: weight. That was the thing about shopping. The dressing room could be a dangerous place. The usual dressing room question on both of our lips: *Does this make me look fat?*

For the longest time my mother had seemed unhappy with my appearance. She worried over my nose, which was sprouting a dangerously not okay bump; my overcrowded teeth and uneven bite, in need of oral surgery and expensive orthodontia; and especially, before my latest diet, over my chubby tummy and inner thighs that rubbed together. In the dressing room, she usually tried her best to be honest but politic: *It's not the most flattering cut. It's the wrong shape for you. That style can be hard to carry off. It does you no favors. You can do better.* I said the same back to her. When something looked good, or good enough, we were relieved. We rejoiced. And we bought. But the subterranean insults masquerading as helpful hints stung. I hoped all that would change now that I was thinner.

We drove from Rockville Centre through the ragged poverty of the bordering town of Hempstead, passing a stark invisible line between black and white, poor and rich, and crossed into Garden City, where large grand houses sat on swaths of green lawn.

Turning on the soft-rock station, my mother hummed along to Simon and Garfunkel's "Bridge over Troubled Water." This was her all-time favorite song. I listened to the lyrics. Who was the bridge? And the friend sailing right behind? Not my brothers and me. My father? How could that be? Or was the bridge God, and was she dreaming for herself something better in the afterlife? When would it be my mother's time to shine?

When I was nine, there'd been an HBO broadcast of the reunion concert in Central Park. My mother had let me stay up late to watch. Art Garfunkel was bohemian cool, with his white button-down shirt and rolled-up sleeves worn under a vest and tucked into faded femme jeans. Paul Simon sang next to him in suit trousers and a blazer with a T-shirt, as if he and Art had the one suit between them for the evening. I wanted to be just like them. I wanted to be an artist and sing to the rooftops about cigarettes and cross-country bus trips and love affairs. I tried to imagine my mother and father in college and at a diner or sitting on a twin bed, listening to records together. I tried hard to love them.

When Marvin Gaye's "Sexual Healing" came on, she abruptly turned the radio off.

"Why can't I listen?" I wanted to know.

"You're too young for that."

After driving past the residential neighborhoods, we came to the department store. We parked in the large lot and made sure our doors were locked and the windows rolled up.

Then we entered the hush and hum of the modern and milky-white first floor, past the Shiseido counter, where my mother sometimes treated herself to makeup and moisturizers sold by an older Japanese lady with perfect skin, past the handbags and scarves and hosiery sections and the shoe department. We glided up the escalator to the preteen department.

We usually didn't shop here, not for me. Sale or no, Bloomingdale's was expensive, and by budgetary necessity, my mother preferred bargains. Today, though, we'd splurge.

I headed straight to the rack of Esprit clothes along a back wall. I was obsessed with their catalogs. Their models were "real" people, creative city types who were styled in carefree, colorful cotton. All of the models, including the children, appeared to live in loft apartments, the kind you got to by freight elevator. The clothes were just vaguely preppy enough for my mother and recognizably artsy enough for me. I piled hanger after hanger over my arm, and my mother did, too, until we couldn't carry anything more.

We both took a number, the highest available, and headed into a fitting room. My mother sighed, taking a seat.

As I undressed, stripping off everything but my saggy underwear and cotton training bra, my mother inspected me with approval. Then I started trying things on.

I couldn't believe it. A miracle! The clothes looked good. All of them.

My mother went wild, relieved to see me pretty, and bought me a lavish capsule wardrobe. She drew the line at the days-of-the-week underwear I pined for that came in a plastic pack. I didn't care; I was ecstatic. We selected a canary-yellow short-sleeved cotton minidress with a wide belt, a navy sweater I planned to tie around my shoulders, and best of all, a red paisley tunic-length blouse paired with stretchy black stirrup pants that I'd wear along with my black rubber and sparkly rhinestone Madonna bracelets for the variety show at school. The year before, I'd sung "Out Here on My Own," from *Fame*. This time I'd be performing "Can't Fight This Feeling" by REO Speedwagon.

"Don't tell your father," my mother made me swear as the purchases were added up at the register. She tapped her credit card on the counter before handing it over to the salesclerk. We couldn't risk making him mad. He was just as likely to be happy for me to have the new clothes as angry with my mother for spending all that money, but there was no way to be sure.

"Receipt in the bag?"

"I'll take the receipt with me," my mother said, stuffing it into the back of her wallet.

We stopped in for her at the sale in the women's department. I was used to weekend afternoons watching her scrutinize the racks; she'd expertly move hangers from right to left and pass quick judgments, trying on her selections while I sat on the dressing room bench with her street clothes heaped on my lap. But she didn't feel like shopping for herself today. Maybe we'd spent enough. Maybe she didn't want to ruin things by feeling fat.

Instead, my mother guided me toward the cosmetic department on the main floor.

"I think you're old enough to wear makeup." What? I couldn't believe it, but there she was, leading me to the Clinique counter.

"Only blush and lip gloss for now." She had me sit on the makeup stool and asked for the lightest shade of each. My legs dangled while she taught me how to fake-smile to make the apples of my cheeks pop so I'd know where to leave the faint dash of pink. This was how she mothered me.

"Just a little," she said. "You're thirteen. You want to look natural, not cheap." I considered what that might mean.

Afterward, we sat across from one another at a nearby diner and ordered a diet soda and diet platter each. The platters came with ice-cream-shaped scoops of tuna salad and egg salad and cottage cheese. Conversation between us was strained. She talked about overly permissive parents, men who drank too much, Jews with Christmas trees. She handed me nickels and dimes and asked me to go feed the meter. It was cold out, but the sun was bright, and I blocked it with my forearm. I made my way back to the table, and we tried halfheartedly gossiping about my brothers and their friends. When we ran out of things to say, we talked about my new clothes or the things she wanted. Once my parents had the money, she bought herself diamond stud earrings and a Torah scroll pendant that hung on a gold chain, and had her engagement ring reset and arranged on a bed of diamond chips. She bought me clothes and paid for summer camp. My mother believed wholeheartedly in the power of nice things to make us happy.

*　　*　　*

The summer before ninth grade, though I wasn't remotely athletic, I signed up for a bike trip with the 92nd Street Y. We'd spend a couple of weeks cycling our way through Martha's Vineyard and Cape Cod and Nantucket. I sometimes had to get off and walk my bike, and on most rides I was the last camper to arrive. But I loved racing down hills, working the brakes, and the long flat afternoons when I couldn't see anyone in front of me or behind me and could feel my calf muscles taking shape. Until one day, when I was waiting at a stoplight outside a supermarket parking lot for the girl following me. A man drove up and honked, rolling down his window. It was hot, bright sun on asphalt. I figured he wanted directions, and I was about to say I wasn't from around there when I saw something poking

out from his short shorts, huge and pink. He had his hand
on it. I wanted to throw up. I'd never seen a penis before,
and I knew in an instant I'd never forget his no matter how
long I tried. The biker behind me rode up, and I shouted,
"Come on!" and we went flying.

*   *   *

Late that August, my friend Monica invited me and a couple
of other girls up to her parents' lake house. Unlike the rest
of us, Monica was from the rich side of Rockville Centre,
but her family was different from most of their neighbors.
Her father made good money and would take us out to
Benihana and pay with a hundred-dollar bill like it was no
big deal, but he wore undershirts by themselves at home
on the weekend like my father did, and he had a thicker
Brooklyn accent than was usually heard on that side of town.
He was Jewish and technically Monica's stepdad, but he was
her "real" father, the one who had adopted and raised her.
Monica's mom was Catholic and Colombian. She was an
attentive and warm stay-at-home mom who doted on her
husband and daughter and threw Monica a surprise birthday
party every year. I hadn't had a birthday party since I was a
little kid, much less any sort of surprise, so this impressed
me. When I came over after school or on the weekends, her
mom gave me hugs. I loved it at Monica's.

Monica had straight black hair, great taste in music, and
a closet filled with skillfully folded Benetton sweaters and
matching socks. At the lake, Monica knew how to drive their

small boat, and her father let us go out on the water without him. It was the first time I'd been on a motorboat since that long-ago family vacation in Maine, and this time we were free and far from my father, and the sun was shining on us and I could have stayed on that lake forever.

One night an older boy who lived next door gave me a ride on his three-wheeler. On a rainy day I went with Monica and the other girls to see *Stand by Me* at a mall in Oneonta, and in the parking lot waiting for our ride home, we talked about which of us was most like which character, and how the four of us would stay friends forever.

We started drinking on our last night. It was my first time. Maybe Monica's mom gave us the wine coolers, or else we just grabbed them from the fridge or swiped them from the neighbors. With just a four-pack between us, we took gingerly sips and then sugary peachy swigs, and when we lit our first cigarettes, a friend showed me how to inhale and nobody laughed, just like they hadn't that morning when I couldn't get up on water skis. I felt grown up, and hopeful for the first time in maybe forever.

SIX

"LET ME SEE JESSIE," Mr. Goodman said as he arranged and rearranged the student actors at the foot of the auditorium stage, forming various potential family configurations, figuring out who fit. This was the final day of callbacks for our high school production of *Brighton Beach Memoirs* by Neil Simon. It was between my best friend, Kathy, and me for the role of Laurie, the youngest daughter. The fall drama was a big deal. The spring musical had the allure and magic of a live orchestra in the pit, show tunes and choreography, and a large cast and crew. But the drama was for serious actors. Kathy and I were ninth-graders and had gone to tryouts together to face the older, intimidatingly cool theater kids. But now she was my competition. I paced the chorus room with the script in my hand, going over my lines even though I knew them by heart. Kathy told me not to worry, that I would definitely be the one to get it, but I wasn't so sure.

Stanley Goodman, the school drama teacher and director of the school play, motioned for me to walk all the way downstage. I stood in front of the others with my hands clasped in front of me and tried to look the part of a father-less Depression-era Brooklyn girl. Jason, who was also in ninth grade and had starred in my soap opera parody, was there beside me, up for the lead role of Jerome. I stared out into the sea of seats. Mr. Goodman—or Stan, as we called him when he wasn't around—was older, in his forties, but crush-worthy, just like I'd heard, with worn Levi's and heavy eyelids that made me think of the phrase *bedroom eyes,* which I must have read in a book. He'd gone to theater school at New York University and lived in the city with his wife and their young daughter. My mother didn't trust him, even though he'd been teaching at South Side for al-most twenty years. She'd heard that he smoked marijuana and lived in the Village, and she thought he was too close to his students. My hair was cut in a bob. Kathy's was long. I wondered which he'd prefer.

I prayed that I would get the part. That it would be me, not Kathy. I told myself she didn't care like I did, that she wasn't as into drama, although she had played a dancing Indian and Wendy's daughter Jane in *Peter Pan* in seventh grade and had gotten to fly, and I had only been a lost boy named Nibs. Plus, Kathy took jazz and tap. I couldn't move as well, but I could sing—not that the role called for either. We were both good students. I wasn't sure what would make the difference, what the deciding factor might be in whether or not my life would change.

At least you're Jewish, I reminded myself as Mr. Good-man took in the visual of this potential family, hoping that would help, given the play. But Jason wasn't Jewish, and

Cori, the senior who had nailed the audition for Nora, had
strawberry-blond hair and blue eyes.

Mr. Goodman explained that our set would be a two-story
house, and that we'd remain onstage while other scenes were
taking place. His friend from the city, hired as our technical
director, was coming in to build it. I had to get the part.
Please, God, I prayed, *I'll do anything.* Rumor had it that
a girl who lived on my street was playing the same role in
the film version of *Brighton Beach,* to be released later that
year. Looking back, this seems a crazy coincidence, though
it turned out to be the truth. But at the time I didn't think
much of it or really care. My world was Rockville Centre,
and high school drama club was competitive enough.

At home that night, my hands shook as I unloaded the
dishwasher and put the silverware away. My mother cau-
tioned me against disappointment. It was better to tell myself I wouldn't get it, she said. That way I'd be pleasantly
surprised if I did. But I couldn't stop hoping. The week of
auditions had been the highlight of my life so far. Hanging
out in the chorus room while waiting to be called onstage,
sipping Diet Coke through a straw and looking over my
pages, the camaraderie with the other hopefuls, the buzz
of scene work, Mr. Goodman's eyes on me. I couldn't stand
the thought that it could all come to an end just like that,
before it had even begun. I needed Mr. Goodman to deem
me worthy, to believe in me and believe I was good enough.
Please God, Please God, Please God.

The next morning I walked to school early and checked
the drama club bulletin board across from Mr. Goodman's

office between every class. The cast list went up right before fourth period.

There it was: *Laurie . . . Jessica Berger*.

I GOT IT. It felt like the first good thing that had happened to me. I was the only girl in the entire ninth grade who'd been cast. Kathy was disappointed but gracious, and my parents and brothers kept saying how proud they were of me. This feeling, I tried to convince myself, made up for the others.

*   *   *

It was our first evening rehearsal, and I felt teenage and in the know, being at school after hours. We'd been working on the family dinner scene when Mr. Goodman said we could take ten but no more than ten. I couldn't figure out why the entire cast other than Jason immediately left the auditorium and exited the building. Where could they be going? After a couple of minutes wasted debating what to do, I followed, prying open the school door that led out to the brick and slate colonnade with its blue tile pillars and the parking lot beyond.

The cast was all there, taking a cigarette break. Cori was playing my older sister. Nina, a junior who had starred in *Dracula* the year before, was my mother. Andy, a handsome, shaggy-haired, and broad-shouldered senior in a Mexican Baja hoodie, played my uncle, the family patriarch. His mother had written a book I wasn't allowed to read called *Growing Up, Feeling Good*. She traveled around to different school districts, helping kids deal with their feelings on everything from sex, drugs, and drinking to puberty and periods and masturbation. Mrs. Rosenberg had come to my elementary school when I was in fifth grade, passing out index cards so that we could anonymously write questions about tampons and ejaculation and training bras. My mother couldn't stand her or Andy, who was friendly with my brother Josh, but the day she'd come to my classroom had been the most interesting day of my elementary school career.

"Join us," Cori said, opening the door wider for me. Then she and Nina started singing "Magic to Do" from *Pippin,* like we were living in a real-life episode of the television show *Fame*.

They smoked Benson & Hedges Deluxe Ultra Light 100s. I took mental notes as Cori opened a new hard pack and unwrapped the golden seal, tapping the pack down on the underside of her forearm. I'd only ever snuck cigarettes with friends my age, or by myself while squeezed into the small strip of alley between my parents' garage and the neighbors' fence. Never had I casually lit up in the open as if I were at a dinner party.

I considered asking to bum one, but figured they might think I was too young or that I'd end up embarrassing myself by not being able to light it properly or by coughing. It was more than enough, that night, to stand in the cloud of their smoke and listen to their conversation.

Over the next several weeks of rehearsals, Nina and Cori befriended me. I figured Mr. Goodman had asked them to take me under their wing so we'd seem more like a family onstage. Whatever the reason, soon Cori was giving me rides home from rehearsal, playing mixtapes and Suzanne Vega's first album, and smoking cigarettes out the car window, with me in the backseat and Nina riding shotgun. At the Golden Reef Diner on Sunrise Highway, Cori and Nina drank sugary black coffee while I ate french fries with ketchup or dipped mozzarella sticks oozing with cheese into shallow bowls of marinara.

Nina wore black sweaters and lace-up leather boots and had wavy brown hair with golden Sun-In highlights, and when dressed up, she perched a silver bracelet cuff on her skinny bare upper arm. She came off as brainy and cultured and feminine. Cori had more of an edge, with a string of adult-sounding secret love affairs. The boys all ogled her because she had big breasts, and she and Andy, who were dating, would sneak into the costume shop in the auditorium basement. Cori and Nina seemed very sophisticated and rebellious to me, but really they were good kids who got great grades, and both ended up at Northwestern.

None of that mattered to my mother, though. To her, Cori and Nina were the embodiment of every devious, extreme, dangerously older, decidedly bad influence imaginable. She wasn't alone in her thinking. Many kids in school and parents in our town thought that the drama club kids were somehow depraved. They called us drama fags, a name we appropriated without realizing the implications of that loaded word. The freaks were a closely related social group, many of whom volunteered for stage crew. They wore even more black than the drama fags, and were more punk, and I aspired to be more like them. My friends and I were different from the rest of the kids in town. We didn't fit in. We wanted to get out.

Brighton Beach Memoirs was a sold-out success. Mr. Goodman said it was one of the best school plays he'd ever worked on. Jason was a great Eugene, funny and natural and endearing, our very own Matthew Broderick. Nina and Cori had a tension-filled adrenaline-pumping mother-daughter fight scene that felt both dramatic and real (even if Cori yelled most of her lines), but I felt safe on stage listening to them, something I never felt at home. When the movie with my neighbor came out that Christmas, everyone in drama badmouthed it. Our version was better.

*   *   *

Then the school play was over. I was fourteen and stuck at home again in the afternoons. After those few months of freedom, my house felt like a prison.

My parents and I sat holed up in our separate rooms with our separate televisions and ate our separate "catch as catch can" dinners or the pasta shells with cold sauce that my mother left out. Kathy had dinner served, complete with protein, starch, and vegetable, every evening at six, even though her mother worked, too. But I was glad for the lack of structure and offhanded permissiveness that kept me at a safer distance from my parents. Once when my friend Julie was over, my father started screaming at Josh downstairs. This kind of thing went on all the time, but Julie seemed freaked out and afraid. We played "Three Little Birds" off her Bob Marley record a little louder.

One night I was reading a book at the kitchen table during dinner. The family rules on this were murky. We rarely ate together anymore. When we did, my father often liked to read the newspaper during meals, and then I could read, too, but on this particular night he wanted me to have a conversation with him. I had nothing to say. I had homework and wanted to get my assigned reading done.

"Put that away," he said.

"It's for school," I answered.

"Not at my table. Not during dinner."

My mother stationed herself at the sink.

"Why not? You always read at the table. You're such a hypocrite."

"Don't you dare talk back to me," my father said. "You're going to get it this time."

I grabbed my school bag and ran upstairs to my bedroom, locking the door as I did each night after dinner, when I'd retreat to the privacy of my room to read novels and listen to the radio and smoke out the window. But the lock was a flimsy one that my father had installed himself so we wouldn't accidentally see each other naked, not nearly strong enough to keep out an enemy combatant. My father ran up the stairs right after me and knocked on the door, loud.

"You better unlock the door or you'll never be allowed to have a lock on that door again," he said.

"Fuck you," I whispered.

He started to pound his knuckles. "You little cunt," he said. "Open the fucking door."

I sat by the door underneath the James Taylor poster pulled from my parents' old vinyl *Sweet Baby James* album and heard him breathing on the other side. The anticipation of what he might do was usually worse than the moment of being hit or slapped.

"Don't make this harder on yourself," he said.

I unlocked the door and ran to the other end of the room, shielding my face with my arms. He hit me with his fists and pushed me against the wall and then shoved me into the bookcase of the white bed frame that they'd found at a tag sale. On his way out, he picked up one of my shoes and threw it at me. Afterward, I bent into myself and cried while my mother came in and silently folded a laundry basket of clean towels. She meant to comfort me with her presence. But I dreamed of having a mom like the Farrah Fawcett character in the made-for-television movie *The Burning Bed,* who'd set fire to her house and husband in order to protect her children.

* * *

The big-deal assignment in Mr. Goodman's drama class was called "revelations." We were asked to expose something about ourselves, something real and hard to talk about. The self-disclosure/self-discovery exercise was supposed to bring the class closer together and help us get in touch with our emotions. Kids generally went fairly deep, talking about self-esteem or family stuff like divorce, at least flirting with the edges of true exposure.

I was dying to talk about my father. For days, my heart pumped loud and fast with the possibility and what this might mean. Maybe Mr. Goodman would take me home with him to New York City. But then I imagined what could happen if I did tell. I pictured sirens and police cars and sketchy foster families. I saw my mother being fired and me being taken away, not to Stan's imagined apartment in Greenwich Village (he actually lived uptown, but I didn't know the difference) but to a juvenile detention center. I saw my brothers having to drop out of college and my father being sent to prison.

When it came time for me to get in front of the class, I sat with my legs crossed tightly on Mr. Goodman's desk and talked about how I had trouble making friends in elementary school, remembering how I sat on the sidelines and read novels during kickball games. Maybe I mentioned my weight. Maybe even my nose. My mother's office was right down the hall from Stan's classroom. Telling was never a real option.

Perhaps I could go away to boarding school, like Christina in *Mommie Dearest*. Two kids from my town had done that, so it seemed at least a thin possibility. Beth, a redheaded academic athlete whose mother taught in the English department with mine, was now attending a New England prep school. And a boy who was bullied mercilessly in junior high had gotten a scholarship to attend a small, progressive school in Vermont. I wondered if I could get a scholarship and enroll there, too.

In the car with both my parents at the end of ninth grade or early in tenth, I decided to ask. We'd been arguing, nothing memorable, just the daily sort of bickering that ended with me crossing my arms and saying *fine* or else slamming car and bedroom doors and screaming *I hate you*. With Mark and Josh in college, I figured my parents would be happy to have me gone. For all I knew, they hated me right back.

"Please, let me go away to boarding school," I said. "I hate Rockville Centre. I don't belong here."

"You've got to be kidding," my mother said. "Do you know how much boarding school costs?"

"I can't live this way anymore," I said, trying not to cry. "You have to let me go."

"Dream on," my mother said. "End of discussion."

"You are so unfair," I said. "You don't love me."

"Save it for your book," my father said.

*   *   *

We had jobs as soon as we were old enough. My brothers began with Pennysaver and newspaper routes. I babysat starting in eighth grade at a house that was straight out of a cereal or floor wax commercial, with the perfect stay-at-home mother, businessman father, and baby girl. By ninth grade, I was sneaking cigarettes in their backyard, snooping in upstairs lingerie drawers, and masturbating to *Penthouse* magazines and a copy of *9½ Weeks* after the baby went to sleep. Soon Josh got me a job as the weekend cashier and coat-check girl at Taiko, the Japanese restaurant in town where he worked. I made a few dollars an hour under the table, plus tips, and at the end of the night, the kitchen would send out dinner for me—a house salad with carrot dressing, a hot plate of chicken teriyaki with sautéed carrots, and a steaming bowl of white rice. I savored the seemingly exotic food while taking in the bar scene, being greeted by the hardworking American and Japanese waitresses who joked and unwound and smoked at the end of the night while counting out their tips in one of the tatami rooms. I needed my own money because I was saving to escape that summer.

A brochure was thumbtacked onto Mr. Goodman's bulletin board for the Ensemble Theatre Community (ETC) school, and a small square notice appeared in the back of *The New York Times Magazine,* advertising a summer theater school for high school students. The brochure said that scholarships were available, and I had my growing wad of restaurant and babysitting cash stashed away. (Ever since my classmate Caroline had auditioned for the drama club musical *The Wizard of Oz,* I'd lost any hope for a lead role at school. Caroline was a professional. She had her Actors' Equity card. She'd played an orphan in the national tour of *Annie* and had even understudied the lead role. And she'd been on an episode of *Reading*

Rainbow.) My parents weren't sure they should let me go, but in the spring I filled out the application anyway. Mr. Goodman wrote me a letter of recommendation, and I answered essay questions about my strengths and weaknesses and previous theater experience, and was called in for an interview with Ann and Seth, the young couple who ran the program.

My parents drove me into the city, and my father circled the block, trying to find a parking spot on the street outside Ann and Seth's brownstone building on East Eighty-second and York. We walked up four flights of stairs, huffing and puffing, and were led into a small duplex with theater posters on the living room walls, and books everywhere, overflowing out of bookcases and stacked in neat piles on the floor, and a small galley kitchen where the teakettle steamed. Stairs led to a tiny bedroom and a greenhouse office with a desk and file cabinets filled with papers in a balcony above. This was the first Manhattan apartment—other than Uncle Leo's on the Lower East Side—that I could remember being in. Ann wore a floral dress and asked us to take a seat at the kitchen table while pouring herbal tea into mismatched mugs. She and Seth, in a flannel shirt and jeans, briefly talked about the interview process before suggesting my parents take a walk around the neighborhood.

"Go get some coffee," Ann said, politely shooing them away. "Or lunch."

"There's a diner around the corner," said Seth.

My mother, suspicious of what these drama school hippies

might want with her daughter, looked skeptical about leaving me there alone, but my father dragged her off.

Once they were gone, I performed a monologue I'd brought along and then was handed a series of short readings. The speech from Jean Anouilh's *Antigone* in which Antigone confronts Creon; the children's poem "The Four Friends" by A. A. Milne; the first few lines of a Shakespeare sonnet. Ann gave me some direction and had me make a different "choice" and try it a new way. They asked me a series of questions about myself. "What are the world issues on your mind? Where do you imagine yourself in ten years? What makes you mad? Tell me one quality you like about yourself and one you don't."

Then Ann and Seth talked more about ETC. Two dozen or so students, along with interns and faculty, lived communally in a big house each summer, studying acting, taking music and movement classes, putting on a children's theater piece for the town, and working on two larger productions to present to families and the community and anyone else who wanted to come on the final weekend.

When my parents returned, we moved to the living room, arranging ourselves on the couch and chairs. Ann was twenty-six but already commanding, with expressive hands and thick long hair that she expertly rewrapped in a big, loose bun while she spoke.

A week or two later I was accepted and even given some financial aid. Somehow I convinced my parents to let me go. (It helped that Ann and Seth had graduated from Yale.) Late that June, my parents dropped me off in Eagles Mere,

a tiny town in the mountains of rural Pennsylvania, winter
population 120.

We began the day with group warm-ups and ended it
with cheese and crackers and mugs of hot chocolate and
songs and chants and reflections on the day and meditative
breathing exercises, which we called "unwinding." We sang
ourselves to sleep with ever quieter rounds of "Rose, Rose,
Rose" until we were whisper-singing.

Our dance teacher taught us yoga, leading us through
the sun salutations. With Ann, we explored Alexander
Technique body scans and constructive rest. On the floor
of the fire hall, a community space in town, we closed our
eyes and visualized ourselves at peace. I pictured a green
meadow with tall grass, a laundry clothesline with clothes-
pins and freshly clean white sheets hanging, and a wooden
swing under an old tree nestled beside a pond. And me
there pumping my legs high. In acting class, we practiced
the Meisner technique and the Method, and sat in a circle
with the lights dimmed, reading *Under Milk Wood* aloud. We
analyzed and memorized Shakespeare's sonnets and hung
out on the porch. We had music class in the Presbyterian
chapel next door. We marched in the town's July Fourth
parade. On warm afternoons we bought ice cream cones at
the Sweet Shop. We took naps. We went on cookouts. Once
we took a day off from rehearsals and went on a field trip
to a state forest. It was my first time on a hiking trail. At
the end of the steep walk was our own natural water park.
We slid down the rocky waterslides into cool rushing water
and dried off on smooth, hot stones.

A boy named Elijah liked me. Unlike the other suburban kids who came from Ohio or New Jersey or Massachusetts, or the prep school students from Manhattan, Elijah was an African-American boy from the Bronx. He had a body like a dancer's and his eyes were always lit. Elijah wanted to be my boyfriend. But I was shy and scared, comfortable only with unrequited crushes. I didn't know how to like a boy who liked me back. We were cast as the young lovers in an eighteenth-century Italian play. Our director dressed us like 1950s teenagers, with me in a poodle skirt and oxford shoes and Elijah in dark cuffed jeans and a black leather jacket. Onstage, I put my arms around Elijah's neck, and he rested his hands on my hips. We shared my first real kiss. My grandmother watched from the audience, horrified.

*   *   *

The downstairs hallway in my parents' house was lined with posed, framed portraits of my brothers and me taken by photographers on school picture day or at Josh's bar mitzvah or our uncle Alan's wedding. I stood at the end of the hallway and stared at myself in the gold oval mirror that hung at eye level. It was an antique, or at least something old that my parents had picked up, the kind of thing that had seemed luxurious and precious when I was younger. Now I considered myself, alert to the bump on my nose, inspecting my profile from each angle, willing the bump to stop growing, trying to tell myself it wasn't as bad as I thought. My mother noticed me looking at myself in the mirror and came in from the kitchen.

"There's something you can do for that, you know," she said. "I've never told you this. But when I was sixteen, I had my nose fixed."

Her mysteriously ruler-straight nose instantly made sense.

"Daddy and I would be happy to pay for you to have one, too," she continued. This surprised me. They wouldn't pay for the drama club trip to London or the school exchange trip to Spain, and I figured a nose job had to be at least as expensive. "Insurance might even cover it. You'll be old enough in a year."

"What's wrong with my nose?" I said, pretending I had no idea what she could possibly be talking about. "You think I need a doctor to cut my nose off?"

It was bad enough to have a nose with a gigantic bump on it. It was a million times worse to have my own mother say I was ugly enough to need plastic surgery.

"It's called rhinoplasty."

"That's so anti-Semitic," I ventured. "You're a self-hating Jew!" She meant for this to be a helpful, even caring suggestion, but it felt like more rejection.

"I didn't *say* anything was wrong with your nose," she answered carefully, clearly annoyed but not ready to give up. She'd been waiting a long time for this conversation. "But they can shave off the bump. And it will help your allergies. Let's just go see the ear, nose, and throat doctor and see what he has to say. You can do it in the summertime. Nobody will notice."

Maybe my mother was right. I knew a couple of other Jewish girls in school, friends of mine, who had done or were contemplating doing the same thing. I had a bump on my nose. A doctor could fix it. Maybe it wasn't the worst idea. Then why did the suggestion make me feel ashamed and worthless? Why did this feel like another act of violence? I could practically hear the cracking sound my nose would make when it was broken during the surgery. I tried to picture my post-op face bloodied and bandaged, the summer weeks spent in my room watching reruns and recuperating in hiding with the air conditioner on full blast, and imagined myself at the mercy of my parents' care.

I'd never been to a doctor other than a pediatrician. Both my parents came to the ear, nose, and throat man, who examined me and said I had a deviated septum and that most of the surgery costs would be covered by insurance. My mother was encouraging but wasn't going to force me. It was my nose and my decision. Of course I wanted to be better-looking, but the idea of having plastic surgery seemed crazy to me, completely against everything I believed in. Wasn't the inside what mattered? Even if I did hate my nose, wasn't it my job to learn to love it? And learn to love myself?

"I won't do it," I announced after thinking it over for a few days. "There's nothing wrong with my nose."

"That's fine," my mother said, trying to hide her disappointment. "It's up to you."

———

Around this time my father and I sat across from each other in the kitchen. I was reading my social studies textbook, and he was flipping through *Newsday*.

"Daddy?" I asked. "Do you think I'm beautiful?"

I definitely didn't feel beautiful. I had braces on my teeth and felt chubby (again) and awkward (still).

He gave me a once-over, evaluating me. Was he trying to be objective? Scientific? Honest?

"Do you think I'm beautiful?" I asked again, insisting that he answer. I needed to know the truth about myself.

"No," he said, appraising me, shaking his head. "But you are well groomed."

He probably forgot the conversation the next day. But his words burrowed into my brain. If my father didn't think I was beautiful, I was certain nobody else would.

SEVEN

"I'm going to put a PINS on you," my mother announced from the other side of the screen door. I was smoking a cigarette down to the filter on our back porch, my designated smoking area ever since I'd turned sixteen. My parents detested my smoking but let me smoke outside anyway because it was better than having me sneak cigarettes out my bedroom window and burn down the house. My mother was reading the parenting book *Toughlove* and had just about given up on me. "You're out of control," she said as I lit another.

My mother was heavier now, with short wash-and-wear hair and a permanent frown. After teaching she spent her afternoons on the couch, switching between *Oprah* and *Donahue* while grading and eating pretzel rods and chocolate Kisses straight from the bags. PINS, or persons in need of supervision, I'd later learn, is actually an early-intervention government program for troubled youth that aims to prevent foster placement or juvenile detention, but my mother said that PINS meant she'd be relinquishing her parental rights and leaving me to be a ward of the state.

I was an honor student and in advanced classes. I was a virgin, for God's sake. Kathy, who was still my best friend, was captain of the cheerleaders. But according to my mother, I was also a back-talking, occasionally-pot-inhaling, frequently-lying-about-my-whereabouts weekend drunk. My mother said I was bad, *bad to the bone*.

Josh and Mark, away at college, were no longer around to witness my parents' fights alongside me from the upstairs railing, or to keep me safe in their bedroom.

"Maybe I'll tell," I said. She knew exactly what I meant.

Weeks before, we'd faced off on the same back porch, the screen door again shut between us. She'd been carrying brown paper grocery bags heavy with food in each arm and had called me to the door from the family room to help.

We'd argued. I can't remember why or about what.

"Fuck you," I might have said. Or maybe I called her a bitch and told her how little I thought of her or cared what she thought of me. (Though I did care. Of course I did.) Whatever I'd mumbled, whether under my breath or straight to her face, that afternoon, it was enough.

My mother put down the bags, opened the door, and slapped me across the cheek. This was the first time, the only time, and it stung.

Oh, how I hated her. In that moment I believed every awful thing I'd overheard my father say. She was dumb. She was a prude and a hypochondriac.

"Maybe I'll tell," I repeated now.

"Do it and you'll be out on the street, living in the gutter," my mother vowed. I pictured myself sleeping on the edge of the road between sidewalks and cars. "I'd like to see how far you're going to get without us paying for college."

She was right, I figured, and so I said nothing. I had nowhere else to go.

*　　*　　*

I didn't know if I was a person in need of supervision, but I was definitely a mess. By eleventh grade, I was assigned a later curfew and started going out more regularly on the weekends and getting rides home from friends, which meant more freedom. But I didn't have proper boundaries; I couldn't tell a good decision from a bad one. If I was over at a friend's after dinner and someone suggested we drive into the city and the guy with the car had been drinking and was shady to begin with—say he blew up small rodents in his backyard for fun—I said yes and went along anyway. If we then drove straight to Washington Square Park and bought dime bags from seedy dealers and rolled our joints and smoked right out in the open and came home way past curfew and high, so be it. If Monica and I were staffing the Students Against Drunk Driving office and the boys were watching porn, I could yell at them for being sexist pigs, but I didn't know how to simply, politely, ask them to turn the TV off. If we saw a mother at the mall with her toddler on a leash, I would scream at the mom like a returning soldier raging with PTSD.

We drank cheap beer or wine coolers or hard alcohol, whatever we could cadge from an older sibling or a friend home on college break or who went to community college and still lived in town, or buy at the drive-through liquor barn that didn't ask any questions if you had a fake ID. Almost all the kids in my town drank, or so it seemed to me at the time. As long as you didn't get killed in a drunk-driving accident or in trouble with the police at a keg-party raid, it was okay. For me, the goal on a weekend night of partying was clear: Dress cute, get drunk, and hook up. I dreamed of having a real boyfriend, but any chance I had, I blew.

One homecoming weekend, I met an older boy practicing skateboard maneuvers on the asphalt. His hair brushed past his right eye; his wallet and keys were attached to a chain looping from his jeans. He played me the Talking Heads' *Stop Making Sense* and *Little Creatures* while we drank lemonade in his backyard. I'd been forcing myself to listen to the alternative radio station WLIR like it was my homework, so I could keep up with the conversation at a pair of picnic tables called the commons out by the school parking lot, where students were allowed to smoke. The music was starting to grow on me. I liked the Smiths and the Police and Depeche Mode's *Music for the Masses*. But when he pressed play on the song "Psycho Killer," I was hooked right away. He asked for my phone number and suggested we walk to school together, but I just couldn't deal. I didn't like anyone who liked me.

Another older boy named John, who sometimes hung out with the high school drama kids and freaks, had a Mohawk and silver piercings up each ear and went to Nassau Community College. I'd just gotten my braces off. When

I told John I'd never been kissed without them, he pulled me close and ran his tongue against my newly straightened teeth. One night we watched a movie at a friend's house, and he caressed the back of my neck with an intoxicating combination of soft lips and tender fingertips while the other teenagers in the room sat there as if nothing were unusual. John called me, and held my hand in front of everyone even when we weren't drinking, and took me to the drama club semiformal. When we were apart, I played "Just Like Heaven" by the Cure over and over in his honor. But John had a long-distance on-again, off-again girlfriend away at college. They were "taking space" and seeing other people. I couldn't handle the ambiguity. When John asked what was wrong, I said it had to be her or me. He cried and left, and I never saw him again.

I made do with random guys. I would let almost any boy with skateboarder hair (who would never call me, who maybe didn't even remember my name) pull me onto his lap and eventually lead the way to a basement couch or a second-floor bedroom where he'd push himself on top of me. We'd dry-hump until he rubbed me raw, his jeans burning the skin of my legs, covered only by a black stretchy miniskirt and tights ripped at the knee. He'd suck on my skin and leave hickeys on my neck to prove he'd been there. But first there would have to be a kiss; I required that much. And that kiss would be enough to let me rewrite the encounter in my head, to imagine this as the beginning of a romance. One night a close friend's serial-cheater boyfriend followed me into the bathroom. When the guilt rushed over me, I forced myself to ignore it and concentrate instead on the urgency of the illicit boy's kisses, the way he backed me against the bathroom wall and pressed himself up against me, feeling for my breasts with one hand while locking the door behind him with the other.

That February, I went to visit my brothers in St. Louis and stayed with Josh at his frat house, Sigma Nu, which was having a big Saturday-night keg party. (Josh had followed Mark to Wash U.) One of the frat boys was an upperclassman whose hair fell past his chin. He kept having to push it behind his ears. Zach fit my image of an artsy college guy, even if he was living in a frat house with my brother. Josh told me I didn't have a chance. Zach had a girlfriend.

At the party I got wasted. Eventually Zach noticed me. It was freezing outside near the kegs, but we smoked a cigarette and started talking, and then he kissed me. He took me to his room, and we started fooling around while his roommate lay passed out on the next bed over, Zach's sheet of hair hanging over my face our only suggestion of privacy. And then his fingers, one and then two and then three, began probing the inside of my vagina. Which felt weird and painful and way too personal, but I didn't know how to make it stop. This was what I had wanted, wasn't it? Or was supposed to want? The next morning Josh was mad at both of us (Zach and me—mostly me) and said I had to spend the rest of the trip at Mark's off-campus apartment.

I came back home and told my friends the story as if it were something to brag about. Zach's long hair. The dismissed girlfriend, the strange fingers down my underwear.

How he'd tucked me into the top bunk with a blanket and I'd slept there for the few hours between hooking up and sunrise. I left out the part about how the bed had been spinning the entire time, and how he'd taken the bunk below instead of holding me afterward, and how Josh's fraternity brothers said I was a slut.

* * *

When I did well in school, I took my accomplishments for granted. If I got a bad grade, I beat myself up. Sometimes I felt like a worthless piece of shit. Sometimes I hated myself so much I wanted to rip off my skin. And other times I felt a sort of mysterious, unauthorized inner confidence.

My favorite subjects were English and social studies. I was a feminist, and I believed in socialism and communism once I heard about them. I wrote poetry. I wanted to be an actor or playwright or director or run political campaigns. But my parents said these dreams were unrealistic. We didn't know people who wrote books (other than Andy's mom) or plays or made films or were activists. Perhaps, then, I could grow up to be like Mr. Goodman.

But my parents always said the biggest mistake they ever made was becoming teachers. Whatever you do, they said, don't become a teacher.

Maybe I could become an English professor like Gary on *thirtysomething*. I didn't care about making money, but my parents swore I would change my mind about that once I grew up.

"Professors make even less than teachers," my mother said. "And it's impossible to get a job."

Well, maybe I could be a psychologist.

"You'll need a 3.8 or higher in college to get into graduate school," my mother told me. We both knew that didn't seem likely given my math grades, despite my father's attempts at tutoring me, sessions that ended in yelling and tears. "You'd have to take statistics."

"You'd make a great lawyer," my father said.

Arguing was one thing in school; there it was a matter of expressing my opinion, and that was stressful enough. In fifth grade, Julie and I debated in favor of the Equal Rights Amendment and lost the class vote when our opponents' mothers brought in pamphlets warning of co-ed bathrooms. But I resented having to stand up for myself and defend my beliefs at home, where it was all about taking sides and every debate got personal and ugly fast. Even a family game of Scrabble could turn cutthroat and mean.

Mark and Josh were away at college, but on Rosh Hashanah or Yom Kippur or Passover, they would sometimes drive home and our grandmother would come in from Queens and we'd all sit down together. When our grandmother had the energy, she'd bring her two-day pot roast, the family favorite. My parents cooked, too, or ordered in Happy Hostess catering, and my mother baked banana and pumpkin breads. We sat in the dining room on high-backed chairs, ate off my mother's wedding china, and debated until the inevitable fight ensued and someone left the table crying.

Usually it was my mother and father and brothers and grandmother on one side and me on the other. I *had* to stand up to them. I couldn't just let their comments go, I couldn't just sit there and not say anything. They believed in a free market, supply-side economics, and a strong military. People on welfare were lazy. When it came to sex and dating, my mother and grandmother were the biggest hardliners. Being gay was unnatural, suspect, and pretty much immoral. Having any kind of sex other than the heterosexual married kind was a problem. If a straight woman lived with a man before getting married, he'd never propose. Why buy the cow when you can get the milk for free? Besides, women who had sex before marriage, or at least without an engagement ring, were sluts. My grandmother wasn't a yeller but nodded along. My parents said I provoked and pushed. I did. I'd ask my mother if she'd rather I end up with a black Jewish lesbian or a white Christian man.

Other times the conversations took different turns, about money or girlfriends or career prospects, and Josh or Mark would be the ones to leave the table angry and hurt. The undercurrent of the arguments about politics and culture wars went unspoken. I hated my father for what he'd done to me, and I hated my mother for letting him. Maybe my brothers did, too; I couldn't be sure. They seemed to have accepted the violence in our house as normal.

*   *   *

My mother had a few close friends. For several years she and my father even threw an annual dinner party where they'd pass hors d'oeuvres before serving a sit-down meal. But my mother kept them all at a certain remove, and eventually most of those friendships withered and died. Constance married a well-to-do businessman whom my father believed looked down on us. Gail's husband was a tax attorney and occasionally appeared on the *Today* show around tax time, which must have been challenging for my father's ego. Madeline left the classroom to become an administrator and, according to my mother, came to think she was "too good for us."

My father had only one friend, an older psychiatrist named Dr. Resnick who smoked a pipe and lived in a big house a few towns over. He was a mentor from my father's graduate school days, and my father mostly called him for career advice. To me, the Resnicks seemed intriguingly erudite. They gave me a pile of books for my bat mitzvah, including *A Gift from the Sea* by Anne Morrow Lindbergh and a college dictionary and thesaurus, instead of a check. One Saturday the five of us went to New York for dinner at Café Español on Bleecker Street and then to see *The Fantastics*. My father drove that night, swerving across lanes erratically and stubbornly and way too fast. The Resnicks asked and then begged him to slow down and drive safely, but my father was in a controlling mood and refused. Their friendship ended, too.

*   *   *

When I was sixteen, my mother took me to the Department of Motor Vehicles to get my learner's permit, and my father began giving me driving lessons. My mother was said to be the worst driver in the family and had no patience to teach me, so it would be my father who would take the project on, as he had with Josh and Mark. He prided himself on his skills as an instructor and especially as a driver. When he felt like showing off, he could back out of the driveway with his neck craned over his shoulder and reverse down the entirety of our street. He could weave in and out of city traffic using sidewalks and illegal turns. He could steer using just his knees, with no hands on the steering wheel. He could parallel-park with a stick shift into the most crammed of spaces. A radar detector sat on the dashboard to help him avoid cops and speeding tickets. From time to time he'd roll down his window, stick his arm out, and offer the finger by way of hand signal.

I just wanted to be able to pass my driver's test so I wouldn't need my parents for rides. But first I'd have to learn to drive stick shift. The blue 1976 Toyota Corolla now had dents and a missing fender and a broken driver's seat and was the family's spare car, the one I'd be allowed to use once I got my license. I couldn't wait.

My father seemed genuinely excited about teaching me. We'd drive slowly around the neighborhood and he'd smile encouragingly, lecturing me about blind spots and how to use my mirrors. But I couldn't get the hang of the clutch. No matter how many times he told me to hit the clutch and gearshift *now,* we'd end up stalling out.

He soon lost patience and decided I was damaging the car on purpose.

One weekend we drove the fifteen minutes to Long Beach to buy sneakers at the indoor flea market where you could find discounted Keds or high-top Reeboks or K-Swiss. Then we started practicing. In the center of the large near-empty lot, I revved the ignition, engaged the clutch, and attempted to shift gears. The car jerked and stalled out every time.

"You shit," he said. "Get out of the car. Get out of the goddamn car!"

I unbuckled my seat belt, grabbing my bag even though I had just four dollars left in my wallet, and slammed the car door shut. Whatever. It wasn't like I wanted to go home with him anyway. "Dickhead," I said under my breath.

He circled the parking lot a few times before coming back around a minute later, pushing the passenger door open. "Get in," he said. I did. We were miles and miles from home. Way too far to walk, and I didn't know the bus routes. He started to drive. He *never* stalled. *Fuck him,* I thought. *Fuck him fuck him fuck him.*

"You ungrateful little shit," he mumbled before starting to drive home like a maniac.

I failed my driver's test twice but passed on the third try, when I was seventeen. The Toyota Corolla was mine, at least to borrow when I was allowed. By then the ax had disappeared from underneath the seat. *Fuck him,* I thought as I peeled out of the driveway and headed for Kathy's, or to hang out with the "freaks" at my friend Karen's house, or to the diner or the beach or wherever my gas money would take me.

*   *   *

I was in my usual spot, smoking a cigarette on the back stairs off the kitchen, when my father pulled into the driveway.

"I have some bad news," he said, carrying his briefcase in from the car.

I flicked my ash, unimpressed.

"Uncle Leo died," he reported.

Leo's wife, Bertha, had died only two weeks earlier. It seemed completely implausible, the two deaths one right after the other.

"Sometimes that happens," my father said. "Especially when people are married for a long time."

He made it sound romantic. As far as I knew, Leo hadn't even been sick.

"How?" I asked my father. "How exactly did he die?"

"Lung cancer," my father answered, pointing to my cigarette. "It went undetected until the very end. You really need to quit."

I hadn't seen Leo in a long time, maybe not since he'd handed me a check for a thousand dollars at my bat mitzvah, a check my father had deftly taken from me when he'd seen all those zeroes. "That's meant for me, not you," he'd explained. "For your college."

I should have visited Leo more. He was my favorite relative, and I'd hardly known him. I could have gone to see him on my own after my father lost interest. I should have. By then, I was taking the train into the city on the occasional Saturday and hanging out downtown. I might have splurged on a cab or attempted the F train or asked for his address and figured out the walk from the Village to his apartment. But that hadn't occurred to me, and now it was too late.

I didn't cry. I didn't know how sad I should allow myself to be. I wanted to at least go to the funeral, but my father said I was too young and that it wasn't worth missing a day of school, given how much my grades counted for college. Besides, there was some rumbling and resentment over the will. We'd been left money, he explained. My father went by himself.

That was the last I heard or saw of those people from the wedding album. My mother said family was everything. And yet we didn't talk to ours. My father had stopped mentioning his sister, Edna, around the time she moved away. It was as if, after this several-year interlude of trying to reconnect with his family, he was once again an only child.

EIGHT

SOMETIMES I'D TAKE the Long Island Rail Road and spend the weekend in the city with my ETC friends. Jolie lived in a bookish apartment in the East Nineties, an address that sounded dangerous to my mother even though officially it was on the Upper East Side.

Jolie taught me how to thrift-shop. Digging through a bin at Goodwill one Saturday morning, we found brightly colored cotton Indian skirts and a cream Esprit fisherman sweater that I'd wear all through the rest of high school and college, until it unraveled. Downtown, we tried on fringed suede coats that I couldn't afford at Antique Boutique, and window-shopped the shoe stores on Eighth Street. We went to dinner at a Chinese restaurant because they served free red wine with the meal, even to teenagers. I kept my bag, a canvas army-surplus cross-body, absentmindedly hung over my chair and a middle-aged woman seated nearby put down her *New Yorker* and came over to our table.

"This is New York City," she said, showing me how to tuck the bag under the table so that I could feel its presence between my feet.

Eleanor, another ETC friend, lived in a town house be-tween Park and Lexington. Her apartment was many times the size of any I'd been in before. Her bedroom had two twin beds, with loads of space between them, and a private bathroom. The night I slept over, I forgot my toothbrush. When I reached into my backpack to fish it out and realized my mistake, I kept quiet. I couldn't imagine stating my pe-destrian problem in such a grand setting. And for whatever reason, skipping a night of brushing didn't seem like a good option. Instead I used hers, hoping she wouldn't notice.

But Eleanor did notice. "Why is my toothbrush wet?" she asked.

Eleanor was studying photography and had been ac-cepted to Yale, and I was hopelessly south shore Long Island, certain I'd never belong in New York. There were no more sleepovers with Eleanor after that.

*   *   *

Before my senior year, I studied poetry and drama at the Bennington July Program. Julie was planning on going and said I should, too. I spent my savings. We lived in houses together, and I took drama and a poetry class where I wrote about sitting on the tree stump during kickball. My teacher asked us to raise a hand if we'd ever been bullied or felt alone, and every single person did. My friends and I made up alter egos. Mine was Phoebe Rose Winestein, and a couple of kids even thought that was my real name. One night I let a roommate cut off my shoulder-length hair. My best friend that summer was kicked out for smoking pot and drinking, even though we were both high the night she was caught.

When it was time to go home, I panicked. I couldn't face returning to the reality of my family life. My resident adviser was a Bennington college student with long platinum dreads. On our last night, she sat with me on the porch of the residence house in the summer twilight. I felt sad and scared and at the same time comfortable enough to make my first-ever confession.

"My father," I said. I couldn't stop crying. "He hits me." She didn't say anything.

"I can't go back there," I said.

"Just one more year," she said to me, as if she heard this kind of thing all the time, as if she knew just how it was, her arm stroking my back. "One more year and you'll be in college and free. You only have to get through one more year."

* * *

By fall I was counting the days until graduation. Kathy was busy with her boyfriend, who was the captain of the football team and drove an old decommissioned taxi. My older drama friends were away at college. Julie and Karen had boyfriends, too. Monica turned popular. I made a few more trips to the city, but mostly I stayed home, or went to rehearsal, or worked on my college applications, and hung out with Stefanie.

Stefanie and I had known each other since elementary school but hadn't become real friends until the eleventh grade. Once we did, we became intensely close. We'd fall asleep at night with the phone pressed to our ear, catching up on what we'd missed by not being friends earlier. Stefanie was into school and volunteering. She didn't care about going to parties like I did; she didn't even seem to care about having a real boyfriend, which had continued to be my unrealized mission in life. On Friday or Saturday nights we'd drive to Pizzeria Uno a couple of towns over and order a large pie with a plate of nachos to start. We'd eat until we were full and then eat some more and have hysterical laughing-crying fits. We laughed until we cried and then laughed again at the constantly expanding running list of in-jokes between us. We declared it was cool to be nerds.

I was almost out of Rockville Centre and almost out of my parents' house. But while I pretended not to care about keeping my weight down or my social life going, I was an anxious wreck. I was plagued with headaches and developed a nervous tremor in my eye. In bed each night before falling asleep, I planned my funeral. Who would be there, what would be said, and how sorry my parents would be when I was gone. I imagined ways to kill myself, debating slitting my wrists versus taking pills, and considered what I'd write in my suicide note.

In the spring of my senior year, I was stage manager of the musical and waiting to hear from colleges. Feeling stressed out and depressed, I worked up the nerve to make an appointment with the school psychologist, a graduate student who came in one or two afternoons a week. He used an office in the guidance department, two rooms down from a guidance counselor who was friendly with my family.

He had me sit. We had no privacy. Anyone walking into or out of the front doors of the school could see me through the window facing the faculty parking lot. Why had I bothered coming? I couldn't show him the deep cut on my thumb where my father recently drew blood by digging his nails into my skin, or explain that, though the violence had mostly ebbed, it still haunted me. If anything, my feelings toward my father, who was a constant source of stress and tension and fear in my life but also, I thought, the parent who loved me the most, were getting more complicated and difficult to manage. I couldn't say anything at all about the abuse. My mother was in the building.

Instead I pointed out the window to a boy at the commons who always blew me off and was rude to me and whom I secretly liked. I liked boys who didn't like me back, I confessed. I didn't want someone who wanted me. Then I admitted to having self-destructive thoughts. And how I felt comforted when thinking about dying.

The grad student told me to wear a rubber band around my wrist. "Here's what you do," he said. "When you have a negative thought like that, take the rubber band and snap it."

I never went back.

I earned A's in English and social studies and in my creative writing and drama and music classes but just got by in science and struggled with math. My verbal and math SATs were uneven by hundreds of points. In my high school, that wasn't considered normal. The "smart kids" were supposed to be good at everything and take advanced or accelerated classes in every subject. I didn't even take math and science senior year. Every night before bed, I paged through the same book about college admissions to calm myself. *Schools don't want well-rounded students,* the book said, *schools want well-rounded classes made up of talented individuals.*

My mother wanted me to go to a state school to save money and said she'd buy me a car if I did. I wanted to go to a small liberal arts school. I applied to SUNY Geneseo for her sake, and to Oberlin and Grinnell and Kenyon and Bennington and Vassar for mine.

Vassar was my first choice. The weekend I'd spent visiting the campus had felt like an idyll sprung from the pages of an editorial fashion spread, or at least a J. Crew ad. *Vassar is known for their "beautiful people,"* another college prep book read. I couldn't get over the library with the stained glass, the chic students, and the corduroy-wearing professors. The school was a fantasy of beauty and art and cool kids. I *had* to get in. I filled the blank "Your space" page on the Vassar application with my bad poetry and what I thought to be an artistic black-and-white photo I'd taken of empty auditorium seats. Mr. Goodman wrote my letter of recommendation and made a phone call to a former student of his who worked in the theater department.

Meanwhile, Bennington College offered me an academic scholarship. My mother was panicked; she worried that Bennington was a "druggie" school. Bennington had no grades (teachers instead wrote evaluations) and just five or six hundred students, only a small percentage of whom were male, and none of whom my mother suspected would turn out to be Jewish, straight, and interested in her daughter.

She certainly couldn't imagine my meeting a husband there or getting properly trained for a professional career, the two points of college in her mind. When I called my RA from the Bennington summer program, she confirmed that many students did indeed eat mushrooms, drop acid, and/or take Ecstasy on the weekends. "But it's not like you have to," she reassured me. I had only smoked pot. It sounded a little out of hand, even to me.

When the Vassar letter came and I was IN, I convinced myself and my mother that I *had* to go, that Vassar would change my life, that my future would be completely altered by this decision. My father didn't fall for it. Vassar was offering financial aid, but there would be loans and a hefty parental contribution. Bennington would be less than half the price, the same as a state school or even cheaper. It was a no-brainer. He was right. (It's not like they force-fed the drugs at Bennington, and I bet I would have started writing there.)

But I wouldn't listen. I cried, I screamed, I railed at him. I acted every part the entitled spoiled brat he'd said I was. I didn't care. I wanted and needed this escape to another world. I felt I deserved the extreme financial sacrifice, my reward for staying silent and putting up with them. Vassar was my end of the twisted bargain we'd struck: hush money. Then Mark called and said I owed him big-time—he'd talked to our father and explained that life was all about connections, and that connections were made in college, and that Bennington *was* for druggies. Mark knew about worlds none of us had entered. He'd taught us about scallions and venture capitalists. At Vassar, Mark explained, I'd meet a rich husband or get hooked up with a career or at least get into a better graduate school. One day, maybe even Mark himself would pay our father back for the loans. Whatever he told our father, I was going to Vassar.

*   *   *

The summer before college, something terrible—two terrible, impossible somethings—happened. Monica's mother was dying of cancer. All year long she'd been going through treatment, losing her hair, turning puffy and sick-looking and frail, but somehow managing to help Monica through the rites of senior year, from applying to college to going to the prom. To my shame, I stayed away. I couldn't handle the awfulness, couldn't handle death, and I didn't know what to say to Monica. We weren't as close since she'd changed social scenes and gone from suburban punk to preppy, but that wasn't enough of a reason for me to watch like a coward from the sidelines. Other friends were braver. Stefanie was at Monica's house all the time.

Then came the twin tragedy.

Kathy and I had been playing around in my swimming pool. The pool had always been a place where I could escape my parents. I would hold my breath and go underwater and dive for pennies at the bottom of the deep end and make everything else stop.

I was underwater when the telephone rang inside the house.

My mother came out with the cordless phone.

"We're swimming," I said. "Say I'll call back."

"She says it's important," my mother said. It was Jill, a girl who had never called me, not since elementary school, when I used to go over to her house after school to look at her parents' copy of *The Joy of Sex*. I wrapped a towel around myself and took the phone.

There had been a car accident. Stefanie's mother was dead.

No. It wasn't possible. *No!* Even my father said so when I hung up the phone and repeated the words aloud. Stefanie's mother, dead.

"No," he said, "that can't be. You've got it wrong. You mean Stefanie's grandmother died, you must mean grand-mother. You must have heard wrong."

I wondered and doubted myself, too. The kitchen was spinning. I wanted him to be right, but no, Jill had definitely said *mother*. It couldn't be; it wasn't fair. Stefanie's mom was energetic and warm, giving and funny. She'd always struck me as the best kind of mother.

"Let's pretend it didn't happen," I begged Kathy. "Just for ten minutes."

She nodded solemnly. We got back in the pool and finished our game. Kathy was the swim coach and I was her star diver, preparing for the Olympics. Then we got out and dried off. It felt like we left our childhood in that water. Soon—maybe that same day, or more likely the next, the timing is a blur—we went to Stefanie's and sat on her bed along with her other close friends. Monica called from Spain, where she'd gone to stay with a family friend for the summer after her mother's funeral. At the cemetery Karen held me as we stood in the dirt, and I felt guilty for shaking and crying as much as I did, as if I were trying to call attention to myself, but I couldn't stop.

For the week after the funeral, the family sat *shiva*. Stefanie's family had been active members of the synagogue. Men from B'nai came over to make a minyan, a prayer quorum, so that Stefanie's father and younger brother could say the Mourner's Kaddish. There were coverings on all the mirrors, and small cardboard boxes for Stefanie and her father and brother and grandmother to sit on if they wanted; there were tranquilizers to take. Stefanie wore a black ribbon pinned to her top.

I wanted to be with her as she sat in her bedroom. My mother made me return to work at the insurance company where I had a summer job as a file clerk. The company was owned by Jill's father and he would have understood, they were family friends with Stefanie's parents, but my mother said I couldn't risk losing the job, that I needed the money for college. I hid in the dark aisles of the basement file room and cried until it was time to go back to Stefanie's house.

I resented my mother for that, and for all the other times she hadn't understood me or what I felt was important, but at the same time I didn't want her to be the one who was dead. That past spring she'd been rushed to the hospital from school. The diagnosis was unclear. She'd felt faint, she'd had bleeding and chest pain, she had high blood pressure (which she took pills for); she was approaching menopause and was at risk for developing type 2 diabetes.

But she wasn't dying, she just needed to lose weight and exercise and eat better. Even so, I couldn't sleep at night, thinking about Monica's mom, and Stefanie's mom, and mine, wondering what was worse, a good dead mother or a bad alive one.

NINE

MY PARENTS AND I pulled through the gates of Vassar College in our Toyota van and entered another world, one of turrets and ivy and beautiful, almost grown children. I wore a plain black pocket T-shirt from the Gap, inexpertly cut-off thigh-length denim shorts, a Debbie Gibson–style black bowler hat, and an extra twenty pounds.

On our third round of carrying boxes up the stairs into my dorm room, we saw them: Franny, her mother, Claire, and Claire's live-in boyfriend, Sam. They seemed a different species. Franny was a muse in the making. She was delicate, skinny, disorganized, and brought suitcases crammed with vintage blazers, wool miniskirts, and cream silk blouses. She had wavy brown hair, Dr. Martens, perfectly worn-in Levi's, and a pair of Bakelite plastic bracelets around her slender wrists. Claire was spritelike, an artist with a pixie haircut in shiny black wide-legged pants she'd sewn herself. Sam was younger, in his late thirties, and wore sneakers and a hoodie. Franny's father, I'd soon learn, used to write an ultra-hip nightlife column, and lived downtown. Weeks later, Franny shyly showed me a photo of herself as a child sitting on Andy Warhol's lap. Her family was what my mother, in her color-coordinated teacher outfit, and my father, in his sensible Rockport walking shoes and Dockers chinos, called bohemian.

Franny and I approached each other awkwardly. We'd spoken on the phone earlier that August but only once; I'd dropped a note off with her doorman, and she'd called. At my parents' prodding, I'd asked if she might want to go 50/50 on dorm room essentials. Sitting on my childhood bed, I'd started down my list. An answering machine? A refrigerator?

"A refrigerator?" She'd laughed. Her lack of concern felt revolutionary. "What music do you like?" she asked, her one question. A test, I realized.

"The Smiths," I answered. "Depeche Mode? Um, James Taylor."

"Oh," she said noncommittally.

Now we were here, together. She tacked up a Bell Biv DeVoe poster and played a Jimmy Cliff album, *The Harder They Come,* on her record player. I tried to decipher this new formulation of cool. Vassar had fewer than twenty-four hundred students, just twice as many as had attended my high school. We had the run of a pristine campus with tennis courts, a lake, chapel, dorms that looked straight out of the English countryside, and the most beautiful college library in the country. Franny knew everyone already, or at least it seemed that way.

Franny had gone to the best private schools, and she was descended from the *Mayflower* Pilgrims and a wealthy blue-blood family (though her trust fund had dried up and she was on financial aid, like me). While I'd been at suburban keg parties, Franny had spent her teenage years at downtown clubs.

Vassar attracted similarly well-connected New York City kids who were artistic and intellectually curious—good but not necessarily workaholic students who'd crossed paths at interschool parties and beach houses. And here they were, knocking on the door of my room to see Franny. By the time we'd unpacked, tall skinny boys at the peak of their sexiness, with baseball caps and one-hitters, were sprawled on her bed, playing conscious hip-hop on my pink portable stereo. The sound track of freshman year was A Tribe Called Quest's debut album: "Bonita Applebum" and "Can I Kick It" and "I Left My Wallet in El Segundo."

As part of our financial aid packages, Franny and I had work-study jobs, but they were genteel old-fashioned ones that wouldn't interfere with classes or socializing. I served afternoon tea in the Rose Parlor on the second floor of Main Building. Franny made posters for the career counseling office and could work from anywhere, so she'd join me. We'd bill $4.50 an hour while sitting on Victorian settee couches, a grand piano by the window and the timeworn carpet in college maroon. Franny traced letters onto her poster boards before committing to colored marker or black Sharpie. With my reading sprawled out beside me, I checked the hot-water levels in the tea urn and refreshed the cookie plate on the quarter hour.

Unexpectedly, we became fast and best friends. In those

long nowhere-else-to-be afternoons, we'd start up our conversation wherever we'd last left off. Since we were together more than we were apart, our reports were on the smallest, most intimate scale: what happened in class, on the way from class, what happened the summer before seventh grade. We had existential conversations, too, about who we were and who we wanted to be in the world. Money, we felt, was not the goal. What was, then? Love? Goodness? Beauty?

Franny was taking the famous Vassar art history survey, a math class, and beginning Spanish. I had introduction to theater, a Shakespeare course, and American politics. Together we signed up for intro to sociology. We took ourselves and, on occasion, our studies seriously. That first year I went home for the Jewish holidays with a thin copy of *The Yellow Wallpaper* and a fat copy of Émile Durkheim's *Suicide,* which I read on the family room couch, to my grandmother's dismay. Franny and I listened over and over to the music we could agree on—cassettes of the Police, Talking Heads, Squeeze's *Cool for Cats,* Bob Marley, that Jimmy Cliff record, and lots of early R.E.M. Our room was kept warm, all the campus buildings were, and we'd go around shedding and donning layers. Franny signed up for drawing and painting classes and carried her oversize sketchpad across campus. She didn't bother getting the charcoal out from under her fingernails and was always doodling in her notebooks. She wore her hair back off her face in barrettes. The vintage jackets and the wool skirts and the cream blouses stayed in our closet; instead she put on the same Levi's and two thin wool sweaters layered under a blue zip-up sweatshirt that reminded me of the kind my father wore. In our room with a cigarette in one hand, she'd draw micro-universes in shades of gray. Sometimes she'd draw me.

We smoked everywhere: in our rooms, in the large smoking section of the dining hall, in the bar, on the steps in front of the library. Franny smoked Marlboro Lights, and I got used to the taste and switched my brand to hers, sometimes even daring to charge entire cartons at the school bookstore on my student account, which was paid for by my parents and to be used for books and tampons and toothpaste. The cigarettes were itemized under "miscellany."

We bought cheap forties of beer to drink before going out, to save ourselves money and the effort of waiting on long lines at the kegs. When Franny drank, she was sweet beyond measure. At parties, affectionate and giggly, she'd sit cross-legged in a corner and focus in on me for the umpteenth time that day. Unlike a boy, who might talk to me when drunk or high while scanning the room for better options, her attentions were unflagging. We'd wake up together and go to breakfast at the dining hall, walk each other to class, meet at the library, make plans for dinner and for later on at the campus bar. We'd part and meet and part and meet again. We fell asleep talking and woke up with more to say. When she found an older boyfriend with a single room, she made a point to spend some nights at home with me. With Franny, I came to feel safe, chosen, awash in friendship, companionship, and love. These were new feelings.

In our room, with the beds pushed along opposite walls and our heads still only a few feet apart, we told each other our life stories. Her parents' divorce, our respective family money problems. As another late-night talk session edged toward dawn, each of us smoking in our bed, I decided I would do it. I would tell Franny the truth about my father. I had never told a friend before.

"If I tell you something," I asked, "something about my father, will you promise not to hate him?"

She nodded.

I took a deep breath. "My father hit me," I said. That's how I formulated the problem in my mind. It was easier to think about and say *hit* than *abused*. I put it in the past tense like that—*hit* rather than *hits*—because 1) the violence had pretty much stopped by then, and it had been a while since he'd done anything worse than yell or threaten; and 2) I thought it sounded better, like I'd already put the problem behind me.

"What?" Franny said, startled, reaching for another cigarette. Her father hadn't been around much after he and her mother had separated when Franny was two. But I could tell by her voice, and the way she looked at me from across the width of that narrow room, reevaluating me, that she thought this was a much bigger deal. I hadn't realized before that it would be.

Franny was sympathetic and asked the right questions but didn't judge or question why I accepted my parents' money and kept up the front of having a happy family. We were used to imperfect fathers, to pretending that everything was fine when it wasn't.

———

Franny's father wrote an essay for a magazine about their relationship. She'd gone to the city for the photo shoot but was embarrassed about the piece now that it was actually coming out. We walked to the college bookstore for a copy and read it on the checkout line. He described being a shitty, absent father until Franny was in high school and old enough to go out clubbing with him. He mentioned that she sometimes went to sleep in her clothes and slept until the afternoon. She was mortified but also half flattered. I understood. I knew the familial trick of scraping off the bad, humiliating parts of an experience. Her father was a famous writer. Her photograph was in a magazine. I bought my own copy and brought it home to impress my family.

*   *   *

Semesters passed. Intimidated by the classically beautiful, waiflike girls with creamy complexions and oatmeal-colored hair looking over their lines while waiting for their names to be called at auditions, I gave up on being a theater major. I wasn't meant to be onstage after all, I decided. I couldn't compete. I'd rather be in the library reading and avoiding rejection. I'd rather be with Franny and the rest of our friends, drinking and talking all night.

Franny didn't judge me for my failure. I took women's studies, personality theory, modern dance, abnormal psych, a class on gender and colonialism. She studied Caravaggio and began an independent study on Chicano mural art. We read Virginia Woolf and bell hooks and Hannah Arendt and Audre Lorde and John Berger and Adrienne Rich and Susan Sontag and Karl Marx. Together we took a class on the 1960s, and later, a philosophy course on love.

During those four years, I spent more time with Franny than I'd ever spent with anyone outside my family—more, considering the difference between a shut door and a shared room. We even became depressed at the same time: Who could go the longest number of days without showering, without shampooing? Who could stay in studying more than two nights in a row? We egged each other on, whether to drink more or to get better grades. We read our papers aloud to each other. We got bronchitis and kept on smoking anyway. When my father cursed or threatened me, I held the phone up so she could hear. She shook her head, reminding me that *he* was the crazy one, not me. Franny was appalled that my father would ever have laid a hand on me, and I loved her for her indignation. We made pacts. She read to me from her journals, and I confessed what I'd been afraid to write in mine. Then my nightmares started up, nightmares that would plague me for the next twenty years. I dreamed of my father chasing me with a knife, of my father coming to kill me. I'd wake up soaked and screaming. Franny was there to comfort me.

Along with the rest of our friends, we'd jump up and down on our single beds and sing and dance at two in the morning to Billy Joel's "All for Leyna" or the Violent Femmes' "Blister in the Sun." We'd sprawl on a couch in the turrets of the college library, holed up in the reading rooms there, alternating between studying and intimacies. In the dorm, we procrastinated on our papers in the early-morning hours and pulled all-nighters, talking through our problems with our tight-knit group. We'd lie on a bed together, two or three or four girls at a time, sharing family secrets. One father had done time in federal prison for a white-collar crime.

Late one night, my head on a friend's lap, I decided to say something. I felt cocooned by them, protected and safe and far away from my family. Franny knew my secret, but the others didn't.

"My father abused me," I told them. I had gained confidence by then. Their eyes widened. "Physically," I rushed to add.

I played down even this confession. It wasn't like he'd raped me. He hadn't ever broken a bone or sent me to the emergency room. I hadn't been locked in a closet, or deprived of food, or choked until I passed out, or made to bleed until I lost consciousness. It wasn't that big a deal.

"He's changed, though . . . I think." I wavered. Maybe I'd miscalculated. Maybe this was a mistake. "He wouldn't do that to me now. He hasn't hit me in over a year."

My girlfriends smoothed my hair. I wanted them to know I still loved him. I didn't want them to act weird on parents' weekend. Though I ached to talk about my childhood and needed my friends to take my side, I couldn't stand to have any of them hate my father, not even Franny, in part because that meant I'd no longer pass as a "normal" person, with parents who loved me.

* * *

I found out the truth about my great-uncle Leo during a phone conversation with Josh in my freshman year. Either Josh forgot that I hadn't been told or he figured I should have been.

Uncle Leo hadn't died of lung cancer after all, Josh said. Leo had hanged himself.

I couldn't believe it. Leo had committed suicide in his seventies, after escaping the Nazis, moving to New York, and devoting himself to taking care of Bertha. Everyone in my family knew but me. So that was why I hadn't been allowed to go to the funeral, I realized, furious at my father for deceiving me. Mostly, I couldn't stop picturing Leo hanging by a rope in his apartment.

When I called my parents and asked why they'd kept this from me, they said at sixteen I was too young to handle the truth. They'd lied in order to protect me, they explained. Maybe they didn't want to put any ideas into my head.

* * *

Back home in Rockville Centre over Thanksgiving or Christmas break, I wanted to tell Kathy about my father but was scared of what she'd say or think. Would she believe me? We were in her room, sitting on her bed. She listened and went pale. Kathy had known it was bad, that something was off about my father and family, but she hadn't realized just how bad. She didn't know about the hitting.

"Please forgive me?" she said. She hugged me for a long time, and together we cried.

* * *

Mark asked a girl to marry him at the end of my freshman year. Abigail had gone to an exclusive Manhattan private school but ended up at Washington University rather than Sarah Lawrence or Smith after she'd secretly bailed on the SATs twice. She dressed in long flowered Putumayo dresses, or in plain mom jeans paired with seasonally themed sweaters, worn with the barest minimum of irony. She said things like *yessireebobdoodle,* and none of us could figure out if she was joking, but it seemed she wasn't. Abigail's younger brother went to an Ivy League school and was into juggling. Their family lived on Park Avenue.

When he'd first started dating Abigail, Mark had told Josh, who had told me, that she was rich. Really, really rich. The family apartment was a vast and gracious too-many-tastefully-decorated-rooms-to-count home in a prewar co-op building with high ceilings and huge living and dining rooms and a luxurious all-white kitchen straight out of a design magazine. The kind of place with fresh-cut flowers arranged in a vase on an oval table in an entryway, real artwork, and views of Central Park. Her parents were vice presidents at their respective investment banks. They served on boards and attended charity functions and had elite name-brand friends and business connections. Abigail's mother came from money, but her father was self-made, Mark said.

Which gave my brother hope that he might end up with a Park Avenue apartment someday, too.

But Abigail was sick. She was painfully, excruciatingly underweight. Her hair was so fine and patchy that she looked almost like a cancer patient. She skipped breakfast and lunched on apples or cantaloupe or celery and ate big bowls of steamed cauliflower or broccoli for dinner. She ran religiously or went to the gym, or both, every day. Mark worried about Abigail's emotional sturdiness but had a warped admiration for the way she could control herself around food, mistaking her illness for discipline and willpower and health, and her obsessive running for athleticism.

Maybe Mark was in denial. I'd heard rumors from Josh that she'd been through treatment, perhaps more than once. Her problems struck me as tragic but glamorous. A serious eating disorder like that was something only rich girls could afford. Maybe Mark had the same thought. He loved her, sick or not. Abigail, Mark declared, was the kind of girl who wouldn't nag or pester or criticize or dwell on the negative. She might even go camping. She was the kind of woman he wanted raising his children.

It was important to Mark, and to our mother, that I like Abigail and that we become good friends. Abigail wrote me letters on stationery, filling pages with her childlike bubble handwriting. She took me to the Frick and Shakespeare in the Park. After she graduated, Mark presented her with the engagement ring he'd been keeping in his sock drawer in Florida, where he worked for Procter & Gamble. Abigail's parents gave Mark a watch from Tiffany. They were to be married the following May.

*　*　*

At the end of my freshman year, I came down with mono and had to leave school early and take incompletes, finishing two papers in the summer. On a drive into town to check my nearly empty bank account, I noticed the sign in a storefront office window advertising summer jobs for the environment. NYPIRG, the environmental and consumer protection group started by Ralph Nader, had opened their Long Island summer canvassing office in downtown Rockville Centre. I walked in and met the two young canvassing directors who ran the office. Joe was tall and greasily handsome and from the UK. Alex was sarcastic and funny and wore Birkenstocks. He was Asian-American and his family lived in Freeport, near the canals, the next town east on Sunrise Highway. He was going into his senior year at Columbia.

We were to knock on doors, fund-raise for the environ- ment, and keep a cut for ourselves as salary. Against my mother's protests about my safety and her concern that I wouldn't make enough money, I took the job. (My father took my side.) It was easy for me, a nice Jewish Vassar girl, to ask strangers for donations on their doorstep. My first day out, my field manager, Miles, handed me a turf map and a couple of membership renewal cards. I came back to the pickup spot that evening with a thick stack of checks tucked into my clipboard, including one for a hundred dollars. Miles laughed, pleased. Alex and Joe promoted me to field manager and invited me to a training weekend at an old summer camp upstate.

Alex sat next to me on the drive up and packed a bowl, passing it around with his fluorescent lighter on top, and we got stoned driving through the darkness from the suburbs into the country, listening to Van Morrison's *Moondance* album. We shared a blanket in the car and gradually allowed our hands to touch. That Saturday night, after a day of workshops and a vegetarian dinner, Alex found me sitting on the porch and put his arm around my waist. By morning we were a couple.

Alex wore tie-dye and listened to hip-hop and classic rock. He'd once had lunch with Ralph Nader, who, Alex reported, had personally told him to quit smoking. He was passionate about politics, and now he was passionate about me, too. Alex wrote me love notes and made me mixtapes and kissed me in front of everyone when the office closed and the regulars hung out and smoked in the back room. He told me that I was beautiful and that he would take care of me. He called me his koala bear.

Six weeks into our relationship, my parents went away on vacation. I'd been the one to convince Alex that we were ready. We took an old towel from the very back of the linen closet and put it on top of my bedsheet. He showed me what to do. Afterward, Alex said he loved me.

My mother found out that we were sleeping together from Josh, who was living at home that summer after his college graduation and told on me. At first she freaked out because she didn't know Alex. *How dare this boy have sex with you and not show his face here?* After a few days, she calmed down. She and my father weren't mad, exactly. They knew my brothers had been having sex with their girlfriends for years. At least I was in a serious-seeming relationship with an Ivy League–educated boy. It was probably a relief to her that I finally had a boyfriend, especially because my family had thought I might be more interested in women. My mother even brought me to her Park Avenue gynecologist to get on the birth control pill.

"There's only so long you could wait," she said on the way home from the doctor's office. "I was engaged when I was nineteen."

But Alex had to come to dinner. That was nonnegotiable.

The following Saturday, Alex showed up right on time in a button-down shirt, carrying flowers he couldn't afford. To him I was a privileged Long Island girl. He hadn't been brought up like me, with a family account at the pharmacy in town where I could charge maxipads and Advil without paying. He hadn't gone to musical theater day camps and fancy college preparatory summer programs, even if I had paid for part of them myself.

When Alex made money at a part-time job, he shared it with his family. He majored in engineering not because he wanted to but because his parents expected him to get a real job and help support the family. Activism wouldn't pay the bills, he told me. He was looking forward to making "forty G's a year" after graduation, which sounded like a lot to both of us. Like my father, Alex was a child of struggling immigrants and the first in his family to attend college. Also like my father, Alex went to Columbia on a scholarship. His mother was a postal worker and his father a draftsman. They were Buddhists, not Christians, he told my mother as we sat down at the kitchen table; Alex and me on one side and my parents on the other, like we were couples with equal weight and power. *Buddhist.* That helped. My mother liked Alex well enough and said he could convert before we got engaged.

School started. We visited each other on the weekends when we had the train fare and the time off from studying. Seeing him after a week or two or three apart, I'd bury my head in the folds of his wool Guatemalan sweater. We'd make out in the library stacks, and he'd go down on me in my dorm room while we held hands. In the city, he'd cook me a stir-fry with oyster sauce in his communal dorm kitchen, or else we'd go to Ollie's for wide chow fun noodles, or to Tom's Restaurant for eggs and toast, or splurge on guacamole cheeseburgers at the West End on Broadway and 114th Street. Walking huddled together against the bitter winter wind of Riverside Drive, we noticed the way the sidewalk glinted and shimmered after dark under the streetlight. On Sundays we had to say goodbye. This was before the Internet or cell phones, and long-distance calls were expensive. When we were apart, we mailed each other love letters until we could have another weekend together. Occasionally we'd argue in a late-night phone call, and then Alex would take the next train up to see me.

———

For Chinese New Year, Alex brought me to a holiday meal at a restaurant in Flushing, Queens. Around a large round table loaded with plates of food, I met his family. Neither his mother nor grandmother spoke much English, but they squeezed my hand and gave me red gold-embossed envelopes stuffed fat with dollar bills.

One Sunday, Abigail's parents came to our house for brunch. The two sets of parents had never met. The day reminded me of the long-ago trip to visit Aunt Edna and her family deep in Brooklyn or Queens, except this time Abigail and her parents were the ones slumming it, and we were the poor relations. Since I went to Vassar and was growing familiar with the type, I was unofficially nominated the family emissary for the wedding season. At the bridal shower, in yet another intimidatingly decorated Upper East Side apartment, I mingled and made small talk about my major and study-abroad plans. As bridesmaid, I dutifully organized the bachelorette night out and went with Abigail for her dress fittings.

The wedding was held at the Waldorf-Astoria on the last day of May. Abigail looked lovely. She was twenty-three and Mark was twenty-five. My parents cried because my mother always said that *a daughter is a daughter for life, a son is a son until he takes a wife*, and they were losing him. It rained, and everyone said that was good luck.

I studied Alex at the reception. He pretended not to notice the unfortunate cut of my bridesmaid dress. Was I actually going to marry my first boyfriend? I wondered if I could ever make Alex mad enough that he might hit me.

*　　*　　*

Alex and I worked at NYPIRG again that summer. A group of us hung out. Miles was older than the rest of us. He was black and liked to rap and lived in Queens. One night during an after-work party, I asked him to clean up a beer he'd accidentally knocked over. Who was I, he said. His mother? His boss? Was I seriously going to disrespect him? I guess we were both in the wrong. I was insensitive, oblivious to the obvious racial dynamics, and he was quick to anger. But when the conflict escalated and Miles called me a bitch and a spoiled JAP and Alex remained neutral, I felt abandoned. I wanted Alex to stick up for me and take my side. I didn't say any of that to him, though. Maybe I didn't realize it.

At the end of the summer, Alex was offered a full-time organizing job with NYPIRG at the state university in New Paltz, right across the river from Vassar. Forgoing the forty G's, and against his parents' wishes, he accepted and moved into a one-bedroom on Main Street with a bay window overlooking head shops and new-age bookstores and the health food store that sold Japanese rice-cracker snacks by the pound.

A few weeks later I ended things, telling Alex I needed to "see other people."

TEN

A METRO-NORTH COMMUTER train traveled from
Manhattan to Poughkeepsie. My trips to and from school
were punctuated by the glory of Grand Central Station
and its turquoise ceiling constellations. Occasionally my
father offered to drive me to Grand Central or all the way
to Poughkeepsie. Though it was hard to turn down the
ease of a ride, and we were getting along better these days,
I preferred traveling alone. I liked the privacy of smoking a
last cigarette outside on the sidewalk, where a businessman
would offer a dollar to bum one off me, and a hot bagel
smeared with cream cheese bought in a kiosk near the bathrooms. And then settling myself on the train headed north,
my bags positioned overhead, looking out the window and
listening to R.E.M. and contemplating the sun, the Hudson
River, and the silvery gray of bridges and train platforms.

During those rides, the station names called out by the
conductor became poem and prayer. Croton-Harmon.
Tarrytown. Ossining. Peekskill. Cold Spring. The rocky
ledge across the water slowly turning into small brown hills
covered with bare tree fuzz in early winter. The dirty blue

shivering river. An abandoned, crumbling hundred-year-old castle on an almond sliver of an island. Each mile away from my family offering another possibility as we entered the industrial country of the Hudson River Valley and pulled into Poughkeepsie. Up a staircase from the tracks below and down to the station with the long wooden benches and the dingy taxis waiting to take the other kids back to school.

When the dorms closed for school breaks, it was time for me to take the train from Poughkeepsie back to Grand Central and then the Long Island Rail Road home. Sinking back into my old self, I crossed town to the underground drudgery of Penn Station and faced the ride to Long Island with the weight of my backpack on my shoulders and my duffel bag on my arm.

When I walked into my house, I let out an uneasy sigh of relief. The family room with its thick carpet, where I could stay up late watching episodes of *thirtysomething* and *Beverly Hills 90210* my father had taped for me. The usual food in the fridge, the individually wrapped part-skim mozzarella cheese sticks for me, my father's Entenmann's donuts and the Sara Lee pound cake that my mother liked, the Ellio's pizza in the freezer, the English muffins and bialys. And on the kitchen table, a pile of newspaper articles he'd clipped for me. Upstairs, same as always, was my bedroom with the stuffed animals and drama club posters. I'd bring home my papers, and my father would compliment my writing and tell me that he couldn't stand to have me away at college, that I would always be his baby.

Once or twice Franny took the LIRR to Rockville Centre

in the summertime, and we'd smoke on my back stoop and go to the diner. She found the suburbs relaxing and exotic, a John Hughes movie come to life. More often, I'd take the train and stay with her in the city. I was learning how to navigate the subway. I'd take the 4/5/6 to the Met to complete an art history assignment, looking at the ancient sculptures downstairs and the European paintings on the second floor, running into other Vassar students. Or else I took the 1/9 from Penn Station up to Columbia (when I was still with Alex), or the N/R to Franny's apartment. Sometimes Franny would give me scraps of paper with instructions about where to transfer to meet her downtown. We'd walk and walk and walk.

Franny's mom and Sam rented a cheery one-bedroom on a high floor of an elevator building. Claire made us plates of cheese and bread and put an ashtray out on the terrace. We'd go drinking in the East Village or on the Lower East Side back when it was still seedy, usually ending up at the same dive bar we liked on Seventh Street and Avenue B. During Christmas break, we'd sit in a booth and drink slow pitchers of the cheapest beer on tap and talk to strange boys while white puffy balls of snow fell over Tompkins Square Park. Afterward we'd come back home and sleep together on the pullout sofa in the living room like children during a slumber party.

*   *   *

Back at school, Franny and I moved together to nearby singles in a dorm with an edgier reputation. Jewett House looked like a castle and came complete with a fairy-tale tower shooting up from the middle of the building, where legend had it that the poet Edna St. Vincent Millay had jumped off, only to be caught by a tree.

From the very beginning with Franny, I paid for things when she didn't have the money—pizza, beer, takeout. Not all or even half of the time but enough so that I couldn't help noticing. Franny waited for checks from her father to clear, bit her fingernails with worry, went for embarrassed meetings with financial aid officers. I wanted to help.

"I'll pay you back," she'd say.

"Forget about it," I'd answer, but secretly I'd worry about my diminishing summer savings and whether this meant she was using me. But she gave me so much. Not just friendship but a new way of looking at the world, a dividing line. People she liked (arty, urban, understated), clothes she liked (ditto), subjects she found worthwhile (interpersonal dynamics, childhood memories, summer), food she'd eat (fruit, fried eggs, cheese sandwiches with vinegar), boys she'd kiss (that one oddly tricky to predict), parties she'd attend (most), activities she sanctioned (library or campus bar, yes, gym or dance party, no), her favorite word (*satisfying*). It was like being best friends with a magazine editor. She taught me how to dress, how to talk to men, what to eat, what not to, even how to write term papers. Franny missed every third class, handed in assignments late, yet received A's and enthusiastic comments. She was quietly brilliant but too shy to raise her hand and participate in class discussions, something she had to explain to her teachers at the start of each term.

She knew how to finesse a paper and find a through line, though, how to impress a professor with paragraphs that built to a crescendo.

We went to the Salvation Army to take advantage of the five-dollar all-you-can-fit-in-a-bag sale. We dressed up as each other for Halloween, me putting those barrettes in my hair. I went on anti-war marches and feminist rallies, and she went to her boyfriend's, where they read Roald Dahl to each other before bed. We made the small circle around Sunset Lake, thinking ourselves on a country meander. We walked to the Vassar Farm, the muddy, open meadows and trails down the road from campus where the rugby team played. I'd wear exercise clothes and she'd bring her cigarettes. We passed a constellation of red outbuildings and barns. I announced that I wanted to live there when I was older.

"In Poughkeepsie?" she said, surprised. She was such a New Yorker.

The Hudson River Valley, I explained. Maybe a country house, I said, as if this were something I'd even heard of before college. I'd joined the equestrian club and was jumping horses—just inches off the ground, but still—at a stable in Rhinebeck.

We'd go for Chinese food at Chan's Peking Kitchen on Raymond Avenue. I'd order chicken and broccoli. Franny was a vegetarian and would ask for a simple bowl of steamed broccoli with white rice and a dipping sauce on the side. It never occurred to me that she might be watching her weight or trying to be healthy; I just thought she was naturally thin and liked broccoli. When we ordered late-night pizza, she'd have one or two slices, and I'd have three or four. I figured she wasn't as hungry as I was. At the all-you-can-eat dining hall, I'd load my tray with bagels and cream cheese or provolone on a roll and a plate of french fries. Sometimes my jeans would fit and sometimes they wouldn't. Once, when I complained about my weight, Franny gently proposed that I skip the daily fries. I resisted the suggestion. I was a feminist and would eat what I wanted.

Deep down, boyfriends and wardrobes and looks and eating aside, we were more alike than different. We were unmoored. We had intense mood swings. Without warning, we became depressed. We could go weeks feeling normal and upbeat and optimistic and productive, and then the blackout curtain would drop. There didn't have to be a reason. Like anyone else, we had good days and bad ones. But our lows were ten times lower, sometimes scarily so. I worried about what might be wrong with us: Were we clinically depressed or bipolar? Franny liked to sink into her moods, whether manic or sad, and ride them out. She could afford to, I figured. Franny had her mother. I only had Franny. I fought against my depression when I could manage it. Other times I succumbed. All I had to fall back on, to return to when breaks came, was that house in Rockville Centre, the flimsy lock on my door and the bagels in the freezer. Sometimes I missed my mother. Not *her,* exactly. I remembered her as always tired, and the cold jangle of her keys, and the always nothing for dinner, and her complaints about my smoking and the mess in my room. But I missed the idea of her, or, more precisely, I missed the mother I wished I had.

*   *   *

Vassar wasn't far enough from home. I wanted to go to the other side of the world. I'd originally applied to spend a semester abroad in Zimbabwe, but my mother freaked out that I'd have sex or need a blood transfusion and wind up HIV-positive. I couldn't convince her otherwise, so we compromised on Nepal, a sliver of a country sandwiched between China and India, a mystical-sounding place I knew nothing about. In preparation for my trip, I listened to Nepali language tapes and read *The Tibetan Book of the Dead*.

My father bought me supplies at REI. Not knowing any better, I let him pick me up an expensive mosquito tent and forehead flashlight when what I actually needed were water bottles and decent hiking boots. The night before my flight, my parents and I went to see *Alive,* an Ethan Hawke airplane-crash cannibalism survival film. I couldn't sleep, consumed by thoughts of mountain passes and unfriendly foreign lands and all that could go wrong. (*Perhaps that wasn't the best choice for the night before your trip,* my father later wrote me in one of the many letters in blue airmail envelopes he sent to my school in Kathmandu. *I wonder how many other kids in your program made the same mistake.*)

The day of my departure, my parents brought me to the airport, where I met the rest of the students flying out from New York. A group of crunchy college kids sat in a circle, drinking from their Nalgene bottles. They had the right sort of expensive Patagonia fleece and worn-in sturdy boots and lightweight body-contouring packs. I sat down and introduced myself as they passed around bags of trail mix, but I felt uncomfortable and shy and went off to write in my journal. *It seems that everyone else is a vegetarian and really into health (vitamins, etc.),* I noted about encountering this new-to-me type. *A weird extreme to the smoking, self-destructive (in a black turtleneck kind of way) people that I'm used to.* A couple of stragglers who seemed better suited for a dive bar than a Nepali trek kept ducking into the smoking area. We were the ones dreaming of drugs and gods.

After landing in London with a twelve-hour layover, we stored our backpacks in airport lockers and made our own cheap London tour on the tops of double-decker buses before finding a pub for the required fish and chips. Sleep-deprived, we boarded our flight to Kathmandu. Half a day and one stop through Dubai later, I saw the white peaks of the Himalayas out the airplane window.

Nepal was like nothing I had imagined. It was so much better. I took in the green hills landscaped with rice paddies and dotted with sheep, and the temples and markets and monkeys. There were rough dirt roads to drive on, and rickety bridges to cross, and families who rode through the city four to a moped. We drank endless glasses of milky chai tea. We ate steaming hot balls of *pakora* exchanged for a few rupees, and vegetable omelets for afternoon snack, and drank from small glass bottles of Coke during roadside café breaks. We squatted on Indian-style toilets with foot treads and used plastic pitchers of water to clean ourselves afterward. We went to sitar concerts on hotel rooftops. Cool, brisk valley mornings were followed by warm, sunny afternoons. And always we were surrounded by breathtaking views of the mountains.

We'd later spend time living in Kathmandu. But that first day we took a short bus ride straight to Bhaktapur, the more mellow and manageable historical city in the Kathmandu Valley. Bhaktapur's Durbar Square was filled with temples and shrines. We bought a knitting-ball-size chunk of hash from a local boy who asked for a new pair of sneakers in exchange. Our program directors and language teachers were holding a welcome dinner. Already high, I came down from my room and entered the candlelit guesthouse. The electricity cut off in the evenings on alternate nights; they were saving the power, our teachers said. We kept our flashlights close. At dinner we were served fiery scoops of lentils and rice and vegetables called *dal bhat* on compartmentalized metal plates. We ate with our hands, using fresh whole-wheat chapatti bread to soak up the sauces. After the meal, we were given blessings and Nepali names and placed pieces of fruit in front of small statues of the deities—our *prasad* to the Hindu gods and goddesses, later distributed back to the group and eaten as a consecration. Then we climbed up to the rooftop of the guesthouse and marveled at how lucky we were to have wound up there. I woke at dawn to the sound of our two male language teachers coughing and clearing out their tobacco-weary throats.

I felt elated by the newness swirling around me. If Vassar was a different world, this was a new galaxy. Sitting in courtyards under the midday sun, letting my cheeks grow warm, I could feel myself change.

In the mornings we studied the Nepali language, picking up just enough to communicate with our homestay families and get around on our own. In the afternoons we hosted guest speakers on Nepali life and culture. On the streets, children called out to us for pencils and candy and hellos. We walked by animals and around rickshaws crowding the road and covered our mouths with cloth. We girls wore long skirts and T-shirts with our hiking boots or flip-flops. Then we left Bhaktapur behind, taking a bumpy bus on a series of ever more basic roads toward our village homestay, in a remote hill town in the far western countryside. When the road ended, we trekked the rest of the way.

I couldn't keep up. Our teachers had arranged porters to carry our packs up and down the mountains (though some of the guys in our group refused the help), but even without a pack, simply propelling myself forward and *walking* all those miles was more than I could manage. I needed a break every ten minutes. I needed water. I needed a cigarette. I wondered if I could make it or if I should quit and go home. I had come to Nepal not knowing how to hike, not even realizing that was the reason most travelers came here. Some of the hardier hikers circled back to where I was at the end of the line, offering advice and encouragement and precious moleskin padding for my newly formed blisters.

There was no way to turn back, so I kept walking.

Darkness approached. We found a teahouse, ate steaming, spicy, overflowing plates of *dal bhat,* and rolled our sleeping bags out on the floor. By the time we got to the village a day later, I had a lump on my head from the bumpy bus ride, wrecked feet from my new boots, lice in my hair, and mosquito bites all over my forehead that looked like a rash of acne. I was blissfully happy.

We spent a few days living in the village with host families, then a night sleeping under more stars than I've seen before or since. That blinding scrim of stars made the Museum of Natural History's Hayden Planetarium show seem like a night-light. Afterward, the group split up, and we were charged with finding our own way back to Kathmandu. I set out with two friends to visit a place where, we were told, old people went to renounce their material belongings and pursue holiness in their final years. Over the next few days, we encountered devout beggars and blessings, medicine men and shamans, and deserted beaches where we sunbathed and did laundry. On our trek, we dug holes to shit in and set our maxipads and tampons on fire. In Kathmandu, I declared myself a vegetarian, got myself down to one cigarette a day, and went to my first yoga class.

We were living with new homestay families. Mine was all the way on the opposite side of town from the schoolhouse, out by the Swayambhunath Monkey Temple. You couldn't depend on there being street signs, so my homestay father drew me an intricate map of the route. Way too afraid to dare a borrowed bicycle through the needle-narrow and bustling crowded market lanes, I walked the seven or eight miles round-trip each day instead. In between morning language class and afternoon excursions or lectures, I drank sweet chai and sat with my new friends on the schoolhouse lawn.

Mail arrived in the early afternoons. My father sent a growing stack of letters. He wrote that he missed me so much he could cry. He sent me kisses; he took care of arranging my course schedule for the fall and made sure that Franny saw to my housing. He wrote news reports about the first World Trade Center bombing and Zoë Baird's "Nannygate" and television show updates and disappointment about how little I'd written in return. My mother, in her own smaller batch of notes, added concerns about my health. *Is the nutrition sufficient? What are you doing about protein?* I skimmed the letters, waiting for the inevitable backhanded remark. It wasn't so much what they said but the tone I could hear in my ear as I read. *We have only received one letter from you. You must be having a great time and are too busy to write. But give us a break.* Or there might be a complaint about their lives. *We had a good time in Italy but didn't find the food as great as everyone says . . . Mom and I are having another romantic night in front of the TV. You really know how to hurt an old couple . . . It snowed most of the day. Mom is worried as usual . . . Daddy and Josh are outside shoveling—so you avoided that one . . .* I couldn't stand these stacks of mail, bothered by how easily my parents pretended we were a normal family. My father's letters, in particular, made me sick to my stomach. My mother's concerns about my health and safety felt forced and fake when I knew I was safer (and healthier) in Nepal than I'd ever been in their house.

Then, on a hike one day in the hills outside of Kathmandu, a friend confided in me about her father. He'd sexually abused her and her sister for years, coming into their bedroom in the middle of the night. She had finally told her mother. Her parents were working on their marriage; they met with their pastor for counseling sessions; her father was sorry. I told her about my family. Knowing there was a worse thing than what I'd experienced gave me an odd courage. (I collected these worse things.) If my friend could forgive, maybe I could, too.

I went off on my own for a monthlong independent study in a village in the middle hills of the Himalayas. I set out carrying rupees and clothes and iodine pills for my water and a journal and *Zen and the Art of Motorcycle Maintenance* and a tiny purple paperback of the Dalai Lama's *A Policy of Kindness* and a Tom Robbins novel, *Even Cowgirls Get the Blues*. With the help and company of a guide I'd hired along the way, I trekked through green valleys surrounded by snowcapped peaks. We stayed in teahouses and walked across questionable suspension bridges that were missing every third slat. Through exhaustion and rain and an unexpected snowstorm I kept going, feeling there was something out there bigger than me, guiding me forward. Afterward, when I was back with my program, we went river-rafting and on a jungle safari where we took stoned naps in the heat of the day and went on elephant and canoe rides in the early mornings and late afternoons.

But I wasn't all courage, and I hadn't changed as much as I would have liked. Back before my independent study trip, I'd pierced my nose at a Kathmandu jewelry shop one afternoon with some friends. I told my mother about it in a letter, explaining that I had learned to love myself, the bump on my nose, all of me. *I feel beautiful,* I wrote. And I did. Which felt like a miracle. She fired her response back, said she was sickened and disgusted by me and wouldn't be able to sleep at night unless I took the nose ring out. *You are acting like a barbarian,* she wrote. My father took to labeling his letters *post mutilation 1* and *post mutilation 2* and so on. I was self-destructive, they said.

So I left Nepal with a hole rather than a ring in my nose, a choice my friends couldn't understand, and a hollow I didn't fill for almost ten years, before finally placing in a small silver hoop and then, later, a tiny diamond stud.

ELEVEN

AFTER NEPAL, I spent a carefree summer traveling around Israel and working on a kibbutz with Stefanie. We cleaned toilets, mopped floors, and scrubbed tables. In the communal kitchen, we peeled and sliced, mixed and grated. Once promoted to the fields, we sipped hot coffee at dawn, climbed into the back of a pickup truck, and headed off to pick fruit and check irrigation pipes. At night, after hanging out at the kibbutz bomb-shelter-turned-bar, I went skinny-dipping with guys who thought me (and my nose) sexy, and sometimes I followed them to their rooms. But when I was back at Vassar, a familiar feeling of depression returned.

I was majoring in psychology and secretly hoping to understand more about the cycle of violence that plagued my family. I felt safer examining this from an intellectual remove, walking through leafy paths under the brick archway that led to Blodgett Hall, where the psychology classes were held, settling my things amid the comforting quiet and slightly musty smells in small, old rooms there. I stayed up late reading Freud. I signed up for a seminar in abnormal psychology and searched the *DSM-III-R* for what might be wrong with my parents and, in turn, with me.

I wondered about my maternal grandmother, Ruth, and why exactly she'd spent time in psychiatric hospitals when my father was a teenager. And about my mother's father, Jack, who'd been temperamental and unstable. And the uncle I'd never met, my father's mysterious nameless brother, who my parents claimed was truly crazy. I had to wonder about my father, too. Was he mentally ill? Or just an awful person? And then there was me. As much as I loathed it, I had inherited my father's temper. I argued loudly and stubbornly with friends and boyfriends. Once, when I was younger, I had kicked my dog, Snoopy. Going by genetics alone, I worried that something intrinsic and unfixable was wrong with me, too.

Vassar had a free counseling center where students could go for short-term therapy. After years of putting it off, I set up a meeting. My counselor, Sherry, had reading glasses that hung from a chain around her neck.

"What brings you here?" she asked.

I was unsure how to begin. Only a few friends knew about my father, and I wasn't used to talking about it openly. Even though I wasn't living at home, my father's grip remained tight. *Don't forget who's paying your tuition*, he'd say. I never did. I thought about it every time I swiped my meal card.

I told her what I could stand to say aloud, bits and pieces about the slaps and scratches and screams and black-and-blue marks, about the name calling and the cutting comments, and also about the many ways he and my mother loved and provided for me. I told her about the TV shows my father taped for me on the VCR and about the wonton soup he brought me when I was sick and about the bargain-shopped clothes my mother collected for me to try on when I came home.

"Your father abused you," my therapist said at the end of the first session. "Physically. And emotionally, too." Sherry said she could help. She thought that by improving the way I communicated with my family, and dealing with some of my emotional baggage, I could alleviate my depression.

Excavating my childhood memories was halting, terrifying work. In subsequent sessions, I wanted to complain about friends and boys and how ugly I felt. Sherry wanted to discuss my father. Each session I allowed the conversation to enter those thick forbidden woods for only the last few minutes. By necessity, though, we had to be brief and results-oriented. Students were offered a limited number of free meetings each year.

Sherry wanted me to send a letter home. "Write to him," she said. "Tell him how you feel."

Confront my father about the abuse? Bring everything out into the open? Was she insane? The idea horrified me, making me feel vulnerable and naked and sending me into a massive anxiety attack. This was the conversation I'd spent my whole life avoiding. Sherry was adamant, saying it was the best way to move forward. And so, like getting a prescription filled without asking about possible side effects, I approached my father by mail, with the plan of offering my forgiveness in the same envelope as my accusations.

I wrote many drafts of that letter, and read a final version to Franny one night in our dorm, her smoking and making last-minute suggestions, tweaking an idea or phrase here or there as if it were one of my term papers.

I wrote something like: *Dear Dad, Please don't be mad. I'm seeing a therapist and she says what you did to me was child abuse. I forgive you but I need you to admit the truth. Love, Jessie.*

He called me. "We'll discuss it when you get home," he said.

I returned for Thanksgiving, heavy and tight with fear.

We sat across from each other at the kitchen table, scene of all those fights and put-downs. I was terrified, not knowing how he'd react or what he'd do to me. I was trembling. It took everything in me to sit there and face him. But my father was older and gentler now. At first he denied and rationalized. He cried. He made excuses, placed some of the blame on me, and downplayed the extent and frequency of the violence. I persisted. I wouldn't let him get away with half-truths. Only then did he get angry, furious when I wouldn't accept his smaller story. His face flushed the familiar red. He pounded his fists on the table. *You were a difficult kid. You bruised easily.* We went back and forth. *You hit me*, I said. *How could you do that?* Part of me wished he'd keep denying it, as if that could somehow erase the past. He regretted what he'd done, he finally admitted. He was sorry. The next day, he even volunteered to go into therapy with me.

Therapy! This was the most I could have possibly hoped

for. But the idea of sitting with my father in some new therapist's office made me want to throw up. I'd be forced to defend myself, and my side of the story, like I was in a courtroom.

I wished I'd never said anything. I wanted to go back to the way things were. They were still my parents. The only people who had to love me no matter what. Though my father still sometimes yelled or cursed, he didn't hit me anymore. More often he was nostalgic and "Jessica-sick" about their empty nest. My mother said he didn't know what to do with himself now that I was gone. When I came home, he took me out for sushi or Italian and listened to my problems and encouraged me about my schoolwork. I sometimes checked my old diaries just to make sure I wasn't making all of this up.

After that, I decided I was done talking to my father about the abuse. What more was there to say? He'd apologized. I was the one who couldn't handle going to family therapy with him. But I needed to speak to my brothers. This had happened to all of us, not just to me. How could we *not* talk about it? By then Josh was living in South Dakota, selling fertilizers and pesticides to farmers. Mark was in Cincinnati, working at Procter & Gamble headquarters. At a Long Island diner, the three of us back home over Christmas and out to a rare meal together, I gathered my nerve. I wanted to know what they remembered, why they didn't seem troubled by our past, why it was something we never talked about, and how they were able to have a seemingly untroubled relationship with our father.

Josh didn't want to talk about it. He made a dumb joke and shifted in his seat. Mark put his sandwich down and edged closer to me on the banquette. He looked at me, ashamed, and nodded. Yes, it had happened. Mark even told me why they'd come back early from Scout camp, how our father had hit Josh and that other camper and been sent home. *Proof*. But I was making too much of it, Mark said. "It's not that big a deal. Dad loves you. You're his favorite."

Shit happens, was Josh's attitude. He shrugged.

I should try to forget about it, they agreed.

The confrontation, I decided, had been a big mistake. I dropped the subject with my father. He'd apologized and I'd forgiven him. It was over. We didn't speak of the abuse, other than elliptically, after that. I took refuge in the typical life of a Vassar girl. I smoked a pack of cigarettes a day, got drunk three or four nights a week, spent the other nights studying in the college library reading rooms tucked above a spiral staircase, and fell in love with a boy who wouldn't love me back.

*   *   *

Benjamin wasn't my boyfriend, but he was the boy I loved. We met the second semester of my sophomore year when I was still with Alex. I noticed Ben the moment he walked into the faculty parlor of Main Building and took a gangly, cross-legged seat on the floor. We volunteered with a peer-counseling group called The Listening Center. I was drawn to him in a way I'd never been drawn to a boy before.

Ben had translucent skin (underneath his pinkish-red

pimples) and a lanky, economical frame. His jeans hung off his backside, revealing a hint of boxer short. At his neck was a leather cord with a crystal pendant that I wanted to clasp in my hand. He wore black Adidas soccer sneakers or else tattered boat shoes. He'd soon trade all of that in for flannel button-down shirts with sleeves rolled up to the elbows, or paired with gray wool sweaters, and brown desert boots, all of which I loved even more. Though to anyone else he might have seemed just a shy pimply boy from New Jersey, to me he possessed a sort of brightness and luminosity, as if he could glow in the dark. Together, I was certain, we were more than the sum of our suburban parts.

We started spending nights together, moving our conversation from the dining hall to the library to our rooms. I broke up with Alex. But when it came to anything more than friendship, and occasionally sleeping in the same bed and cuddling, Ben was withholding and elusive.

While I was abroad, I'd thought about him constantly—while trekking in Nepal, while working in the kibbutz fields, while having sex with other men. I'd composed careful letters and carried his few (sweet but vague) responses with me. I'd poured all of my fucked-up and confused feelings about my father into my feelings for him, projecting every worthy trait onto Ben and hating myself for not being good enough to make him love me.

When I got back from Israel, I called him, breathless with nerves, and we arranged to meet at a café in the Village. I wore a spaghetti-strap sundress with chunky brown wooden clog sandals and a thin crocheted cream cardigan.

"What happened?" he said, laughing when he saw me. "You look more Vassar than when you left. I thought you'd come back a big hippie," he teased, pretending to be disappointed. I handed him the poncho I'd bought for him from a shopkeeper in Kathmandu.

We sat across from each other with our iced coffee. I could feel Ben taking me in. I was tan and thin and healthy, and my wavy hair was long and lightened by the sun. His skin had cleared. We were older now. Maybe we were ready. We went to a bar and spent more than we could spare on good beer. We stopped in at a sidewalk psychic to have our fortunes read. He drove me to his mother's place in New Jersey with one hand on the wheel and the other on my leg, drunk-driving through the Holland Tunnel. It didn't matter, I told myself. If I died with him in that tunnel, I would die happy.

We spent the hours between midnight and dawn talking in his waterbed. I was desperate for him to touch me. My heart was beating wildly. I *had* to say something.

I sucked in my breath and courage, as if about to dive underwater, and told Ben I was attracted to him and needed to know what was going on between us.

Ben said he was attracted to me, too. But I'd had a boyfriend, and then I'd been away for seven months. (An eternity at twenty and twenty-one.) Now he had a sort-of girlfriend.

"She's going to be a sophomore," Ben told me. "It's nothing serious. It probably won't work out."

Oh. I wasn't sure whether to let myself be momentarily elated that he had at last admitted there was something between us, or to hate him for not waiting for me and, on top of it, making me wish I'd never left school.

"Besides," he continued, his face aglow from the lava lamp, "if we got together, it would be pretty intense. I'm not sure I could handle it."

I ignored that last part. There was hope, I told myself. I could fix this. Benjamin was attracted to me. That was the important part, the thing that really mattered.

*   *   *

Franny and I were living in a connected pair of rooms called the Rockefeller Suite, sharing a small first-floor wing of Jewett dorm with a faculty member who was said to be sleeping with one of her students. We had a claw-foot tub and a Salvation Army couch. Franny moved into the private inner room; I had the larger, more public one with the sitting area. All I thought about was Ben and how to make him want me. I stopped eating out of nerves and because I somehow figured the thinner I was, the better my chances were with him. To make Ben jealous, so he could see what he was missing, I kissed guys, including one of his closest friends, right in front of him. My obsession flattened everything else. Ben was all I talked about, putting Franny and the rest of my friends through countless hours of conversation about the state of our relationship. I made him mixtapes. Bonnie Raitt singing "I Can't Make You Love Me." Peter Gabriel's "In Your Eyes." "The Boy with the Thorn in His Side" by the Smiths. We exchanged notes. I confessed everything, told him exactly how I felt, held nothing back. He just wanted to be best friends, he said. Couldn't we be?

"No," I said. It had to be all or nothing. "If you don't want me, you can't hang out with me."

One night before finals during an early-December snowstorm, we started talking at a party and went home together. We drank too much wine. I practically forced myself on him, begging and demanding, my hands firm on his thighs. He and the sophomore had broken up by then. We kissed on the staircase of our dorm, and I moved my hand from his thigh to his inner hip. His lips were there, his tongue, even, but he wasn't. He *couldn't* be with me, he said. Not then. Not yet. He didn't know why. He was sorry, though. "Wait five years," he said. We were soul mates and best friends and would probably end up getting married.

I gave him the most hurtful punishment I could think of. I shut him out completely.

At the start of the next semester, Ben was seeing someone new, a Nirvana-skinny first-year with short platinum hair, the kind of hipster-cool girl I could never compete with, no matter how much weight I lost or how knowing my sense of humor. I'd see them together and want to slice my wrists. Then they broke up, but we *still* weren't together. What was wrong with me? Why wasn't I good enough?

Around this time, I found a small paperback in a Poughkeepsie bookstore titled *Outgrowing the Pain: A Book for and*

About Adults Abused as Children. It was written by Eliana Gil, a psychologist. It took more courage for me to stand at the register in the mall and buy that book than it had to cross any rickety, rotted Nepali footbridge, or even to tell Ben how I felt about him.

I brought the book to my dorm room and read it with a highlighter and pen. I starred an early passage: *It's hard to acknowledge being abused as a child because in doing so, you also admit that your parents were wrong, or not perfect. "Honor thy mother and father" is a very strong lesson, and seeing your parents as abusive may feel like a betrayal of them.*

A few paragraphs later, I underlined a sentence that the author had boldfaced:

It was a problem with your parents, not with you.

I felt guilty and ashamed, seeing my experiences reflected in print. I wondered for the hundredth, the thousandth, time whether I was making too much of my parents' mistakes. This, Gil explained, was called minimizing. There were no excuses for abusing a child, she wrote. I furiously underlined and then hid the book under my bed like my brothers had hidden their porn magazines.

*   *   *

That winter, Mark cashed in some frequent-flyer miles and sent me a plane ticket to visit him in Cincinnati. He and Abigail took me to restaurants and to the museum at Union Terminal and to a Procter & Gamble party. It was a tense weekend. My brother's MBA applications were almost due. (Abigail's parents were going to pay the tuition if he got in.) Abigail, anxious about moving, was struggling with her eating. When Sunday morning came, I was relieved to leave and eager to get to the airport for my scheduled flight home to New York. We woke up to falling snow and a couple of inches already on the ground. Abigail didn't want Mark to drive me, thinking the roads were too dangerous. I didn't want to waste money on a taxi ride I couldn't afford. Mark offered to pay, but I refused. I wanted him to do this one thing for me, to take care of me in that mild Ohio snowstorm.

We fought—a terrible fight. Maybe I said he never stood up for me or took my side anymore. Maybe he said I was being a spoiled brat. Maybe I said all he cared about was money. The next part I could never forget. I knew just what to say, what to accuse him of that would hurt the most.

"You're pussy-whipped," I said. "You are so fucking pussy-whipped."

His face changed in an instant. I'd never seen him like that before, ready to explode.

I didn't care. *Fuck him.* I slammed a door and went to take a shower. Leaving my nightclothes in a heap on the bathroom floor, I took one of Abigail's plush towels and wrapped it around me, ready to turn on the hot water.

Mark pounded on the door, just like my father. "Let me in!"

I unlocked the door. He came in after me. He was yelling and cursing. "You fucking bitch." Then time stopped. Mark was pushing and shoving me. The towel fell off my body.

He grabbed me and slammed me against the shower wall once, and then a second time, and then a third—hard—before leaving the apartment with Abigail. In shock, I called Stefanie, and then a cab, and later on my parents from a pay phone at the airport.

"Mark hit me, Mark hit me," I said over and over. Whether he had pushed or punched or slapped didn't matter, he had put his hands on me. I couldn't make sense of it. My parents picked me up from the airport, and I cried and shook all the way home, repeating like a mantra, *Mark hit me, Mark hit me.*

Mark had been the one to look out for me as a child, to make me feel special and something like safe. He'd guarded me in his bedroom while my parents fought. That he would *hit* me was the worst, most unexpected betrayal, and proved I couldn't trust anybody in my family. I didn't care about anything that had come before, about anything good he had ever done for me. I hated him.

I swore I would never talk to my brother again, but my mother said that was not an option, I had no choice, I *had* to—she couldn't have her children not speaking to one another.

"Why not?" I said. "Dad doesn't talk to his sister or brother."

She gave my father her worst *I told you so* look.

I blamed Mark, and of course I blamed my father.

"No one will ever hit me again," I vowed to my parents. "*You* will never hit me again," I said to my father.

I tried to calm myself, but how could I? I had stood there defenseless and naked. But with my mother saying I had to get over it, I tried rationalizing. Siblings fought. I didn't have a black eye or anything. The whole thing had lasted just a few minutes. But no, there was no way. Not this time. This I couldn't block out or get past or forget.

At our parents' insistence, Mark called me, or maybe my mother or father dialed the phone and made us get on with each other. My brother apologized. He loved me, he said. The apology counted for something, I knew. I wanted things to go back to normal. But I didn't see how they could. I wanted to hurt him back.

"Do you hit Abigail, too?" I asked. That really pissed him off.

I told him he could never, ever do that to me again. I told him I didn't know if things would ever be the same between us. I truly was frightened for Abigail. And would he abuse his children one day? I said the only way we could continue having a relationship was if he went into therapy to deal with what he'd done. He had to be willing to at least make that much of an effort. (I didn't think about my own inability to enter therapy with my father.) He was silent on the other end before agreeing to consider it.

Mark called me at school a few weeks later. He'd decided against therapy. He had enough on his hands, dealing with Abigail.

*   *   *

The second semester of my senior year, I interviewed with a Peace Corps recruiter and was offered a regional placement somewhere in rural Latin America. My mother was not pleased. This was the time, she warned me, when husbands were met and careers established. How would I feel, coming back in two or three years to nothing, with no money and nowhere to go? Having to move back home at age twenty-four?

I decided to pass on the Peace Corps and return to Israel. I'd heard about a Hebrew language and culture program in the desert that would help me find a job there. All I needed was a few thousand dollars for the flight and program fees.

By spring, Ben and I had started talking again. I couldn't stay away from him. My father came up several days before graduation to bring a carload of my things home. He was in one of his moods, angry and hotheaded like I hadn't seen him in a long time. Maybe he was nervous about my coming home. I certainly was.

I was in my mess of a room, stuffing winter clothes in a moving box, when he went off on me. I hadn't packed enough of my things before he arrived, and my *lazy fucking friends,* whom he had taken to dinner the night before, hadn't shown up to help carry boxes to the car, as they'd promised. Ben and the rest of them were *pieces of shit* and *fags*. I was a *selfish bitch*. How dare I? He was screaming at me, cursing, and I was supposed to be spending the summer in his house, saving money for Israel. Kerry, a friend from home who'd also gone to Vassar, was visiting. She and Franny saw everything.

My father stomped out, and I stayed on the floor crying. Kerry was still living with her parents a year after her graduation. She knelt next to me and put her arms around me. "Sweetie," she said. "You could always come live with my family for the summer."

I was too proud and ashamed to take her up on it, to shun my parents and move into a house down the road from them. (And though it made no sense, I wanted to sleep in my own bed.) But I carried her offer around with me for years like a talisman. It was what I had always most wanted to hear from a friend.

Ben was a junior but stuck around for graduation week. We went from one party to another, from afternoon late into the night. Our friend Natalie lived off campus, with posh housemates who had family fortunes that I'd later read about in *Vogue*. We went to a party they threw, and I cornered Ben in the downstairs hallway.

"You have to tell me how you really feel about me," I demanded. "Right now."

It all came pouring out, all the real reasons why we weren't together. How he felt like a quarter of a person. How he felt empty inside, like there was a void where his feelings should be. How he didn't know himself well enough to be in a serious relationship. How ours was the closest relationship he'd had, and he loved me too much to put me through what he couldn't help doing to women. How he didn't like physical contact or being touched that much, anyway. And that we could be so close *because* we weren't sleeping together.

"I feel like a little boy. You're so much more mature emotionally than me. I plan out every move and overanalyze. I turn things around on the other person," he said.

An hour had gone by. Two.

"You should *thank* me for saving you from a relationship with me," he concluded.

He said I used him as a buffer. Ben knew about my father. He said I wouldn't let myself get to know other guys because of the abuse.

He was right. I'd broken it off with Alex because he was able to love me, while I kept things going with Ben, who felt so familiar because he couldn't.

Though I recognized much of what Ben said as true, somehow what I took away from the conversation at the time was that I wasn't pretty enough for him, that he wasn't attracted enough to me, that he didn't like me enough. That we would probably get married one day, but only if he couldn't find someone better.

After graduation, I returned home to live with my parents, as planned. I tried to shut my door and do my own thing as much as I could. Josh had left South Dakota and was living at home again, too. He got me a summer sales job at the bottled-water company where he was working. That summer I went door-to-door, business to business, from nail salon to auto repair shop on Queens Boulevard, until I'd sold one hundred Poland Spring watercooler contracts at fifty bucks commission each. When September came, I packed two big bags and flew to Tel Aviv, headed for the Israeli desert.

That year I learned Hebrew, went hiking through nature reserves in the beautifully stark southern desert and up in the lush green hills of the north; I visited Jerusalem—that city of white, cool stone, with the music of the Muslim call to prayer sounding from the rooftops—and stuck notes to God in the Western Wall; I fell for and got dumped by a Canadian who was making aliyah and joining the army, and I called my mother from a pay phone crying, sure that no one would ever love me; I floated in the Dead Sea; I flirted with becoming religious and imagined carrying a baby on each of my hips and a prayer book in my purse, wearing a scarf over my hair and skirts down to my sandals; I mournfully made my way through the Holocaust museum Yad Vashem and its pile of children's shoes and studied the intricate works at the Museum for Islamic Art; I got a job at a university as a research assistant to a sociologist, volunteered with a group advocating tenants' rights for new immigrants, lived on falafels and tomatoes and cucumber salad and hummus and fresh-baked pita, moved in with and got (practically but not quite) engaged to an Israeli who studied desert mosquitoes and spent reserve duty in a tank, and told my parents I might never return.

TWELVE

MY EXCUSE FOR coming back to New York was Josh's wedding. His fiancée, Rachel, had grown up on the north shore of Long Island. She'd gone to Cornell and NYU Law and lived in the city. Rachel and Josh had met as teenagers during a summer bike trip through Europe and reconnected after college.

My parents bought me a plane ticket home. One-way. Maybe I *was* rushing into my new life in Israel. Ben and I weren't speaking, but I loved him more than I loved my Israeli boyfriend, who couldn't understand why I was so cruelly abandoning him. I felt that way even though Ben didn't love me back. I needed time to think and wanted to try living in New York. Also, I missed Franny.

After sleeping off my flight, I took the *New York Times* classified section and a pencil to the pool. On the phone, my mother had said there was no huge rush to find a job, but as soon as I arrived home, it was a different story. Neither me nor my parents could stand for me to live there with them. I dangled my legs in the water, circling entry-level possibilities.

Josh and Rachel were married in a large affair at a synagogue banquet hall on Long Island. I wore a frumpy black dress with a bow around the waist and elbow-length sleeves that my mother had bought months before at a random dress shop in a Tel Aviv mall when she came to visit, because she didn't want me to have to find something last-minute in New York. I'd agreed to the dress to get the afternoon of shopping over with. But after I returned home I showed it to Franny and knew at once it was all wrong.

Mark was at the wedding without Abigail, who was supposed to be a bridesmaid. He said she wasn't feeling well. I hadn't seen my brother in a long time. We didn't talk on the phone any more or exchange letters. I avoided him the best I could. Living in Israel had helped. This was the first time we'd hung out together since my graduation and only the second time since Cincinnati. He was graying and starting to look middle-aged, though he was just turning thirty.

"I want you back," he said to me. "I'm going through a lot right now, and I need my sister. I need you."

"Then go into therapy. You have to deal with what you did to me. That's the only way to make sure you'll never do it again."

"I can't," he tried to explain. "I already went for couples therapy with Abigail. I can't do it for this, too. I have too much going on."

"But I need you to," I said. "I can't pretend nothing happened."

Mark looked down at his dress shoes for a minute,

thinking, as we stood to the side of the dance floor. I wondered if I was being stubborn.

"No," he eventually answered, more dejected than steadfast. "I won't do it."

My family soon learned that Abigail and Mark had separated after three years of marriage. Abigail stayed in New York. Mark returned to Stanford without her to finish his MBA. Josh thought Mark would be different now that Abigail was out of the picture, but I didn't blame her for that snowy Cincinnati morning. I blamed my brother. He was the one who had betrayed me.

*   *   *

I found a job in Midtown and a studio apartment in the East Village. I fantasized about joining a political campaign or pursuing a career in publishing or the magazine world. Instead I told myself I should be practical, and settled into the first job I was offered, as an administrative assistant at the Jewish nonprofit Hadassah. At least I could get my own place. My father insisted on coming to help me decide between a cheap basement apartment near the Hells Angels clubhouse on Third Street, which he rejected as dangerous, and a tiny, slightly more expensive 250-square-foot studio above a Chinese take-out on First Avenue and Thirteenth Street. I needed his permission and their help because my parents would serve as guarantors on the lease. My father offered to pay the difference between the two rents until I got my first raise. I didn't like the idea of continuing to be dependent on him, but didn't understand I had a choice. I could have found a roommate or moved in with Kathy. Maybe part of me wanted to stay tethered to my parents.

Franny was recently back from Mexico, where she'd fled a bad relationship. I could feel her pulling away; she hadn't wanted to live with me, saying she couldn't commit to a lease. She didn't have a steady job or the money for rent, but I figured it was my fault—that I was no longer cool enough. I had an employee ID badge and a weeknight bedtime and work outfits scrounged from Loehmann's and the discount rack at the Gap.

From my office, I'd call to make plans for the weekend. Franny became harder and harder to pin down. "I don't know," she'd say. "I'm not really sure what's going on."

So instead I'd stand in the back of a crowded bookstore reading, or at KBG bar by myself, or make the shame-faced solo walk to Kim's Video and rent a movie, picking up a couple of sesame-seed bagels and a mini container of scallion cream cheese at my corner bagel store on the way home. Even after all that traveling, I had no idea how to be alone.

When Franny did agree to meet, she'd sometimes keep me waiting on street corners. I'd check my watch and try not to be annoyed. Eventually she'd show up, ten or twenty or thirty minutes late.

"Honey!" she'd call from across the street, waving, a huge scarf wrapped around her neck. "I'm *sosososo* sorry I'm late," she'd say with a kiss on the cheek and an extravagant hug, and I'd forgive her instantly. We'd walk down the street arm in arm, and she'd teach me how to Christmas-shop at vintage stores. Or we'd head to a bar or party. Though she might make us hang out with those Vassar guys who ignored me, at some point in the night she'd turn back to me. Then we'd end up together, just the two of us, at an all-night diner, where we'd eat fried-egg sandwiches at dawn and things would feel back to normal.

I rarely saw my brothers. Mark was in California and then went to Israel to work at a start-up. Josh and Rachel lived in the city, but we didn't spend time together. One May, I invited them to my birthday party at a bar between Avenues B and C, and they showed up, Rachel straight from the office in her corporate lawyer suit, looking afraid of the neighborhood, whispering to Josh with her eye on the door. I was sure she thought my friends and I were some kind of aged-out juvenile-delinquent jokes in our vintage dresses and black boots.

I saw my parents regularly, though. My father's anger that had flared around my graduation seemed to subside, and I grew easier in his presence, no longer afraid. Every few weeks they drove in to take me out for a meal. I sat through these brunches and dinners and greedily pocketed the comforts of the free meal and the twenties they offered me afterward, plus the monthly $150 check to help with my rent. My mother continued to bargain-shop for me at Filene's Basement on Long Island, returning my rejects like a personal shopper. (She gave me her used books, too, including a copy of an Oprah-pick novel dealing with family violence and abuse, *Bastard Out of Carolina*. Her book-club notes lined the margins. I couldn't bring myself to read it, much less wonder if this was some sort of admission on her part.) They never gave my brothers a single dollar after college, she reminded me. I felt guilty and grateful for their help.

They would call me and come see me and have me visit them and sometimes act like "normal" parents and sometimes make threats, and I would slide between rebellion and trying to please them. I tried to ignore the little things: my father during Mother's Day brunch at Bubby's in Tribeca, acting aggressive and rude to the waiter, my mother criticizing my hair, my dating life, my friendships. (She liked my Rockville Centre friends but disapproved of the ones from Vassar.) Sometimes we got along fine. On a fishing trip in New England, just my parents and me for a long early-summer weekend, my father had on the same hat he'd worn all those years before in Maine. I borrowed it for the weekend and wore his flannel work shirt. Mostly I avoided thinking about my relationship with them too much, imagining things would never change.

*   *   *

The banquet hall of the Midtown hotel was filling up with a stressed after-work crowd. It was a meeting of the ACPA— the Association of Celebrity Personal Assistants. After the cocktail hour, everyone signed a confidentiality agreement and placed their folding chairs in a circle. We went around: name, celebrity, horror story.

Several weeks earlier, I'd sent my résumé in response to a newspaper ad for a women's organizer position. Organizing women sounded infinitely better than my boring job at Hadassah.

I got the call at work: "Do you know who Bella Abzug is?"

"Yes, of course," I said, only sort of lying. She was a feminist, I knew. She wore hats.

"You'd be working as Bella's assistant."

My interview with Bella was the next day. Her office at the Women's Environment and Development Organization was filled with awards and framed photographs of Bella and Gloria, Bella and Hillary, Bella and Barbra. A former civil rights attorney, I learned, Bella had cofounded the National Women's Political Caucus; helped shape Title IX legislation, which banned sex discrimination in education; and broken barriers with her bid for the U.S. Senate in 1976 and in New York City's mayoral race a year later.

"I would do anything to work here," I told Bella.

"You would, would you?" she asked. "I bet."

She glanced at my résumé and chuckled. "Vassar, huh? I went to Hunter College, myself."

Somehow, I got the job. My family couldn't believe it. My parents bragged about me to work friends and acquaintances. My brothers were impressed. Bella's former assistant, who'd quit to become a stand-up comedian, offered me two pointers: 1) keep a notebook and write down all of Bella's instructions; 2) don't take anything personally.

Not taking it personally was hard. Bella wasn't diplomatic when telling me I had no idea what I was doing. When she would call from her office—"Get me Lew Rudin on the phone!"—I'd fumble through her Rolodex. Bella would curse, demand, insult. She'd yell or shake her cane, frustrated at my ineptitude. "What are you, stupid?"

As terrified as I was of messing up, I loved the feeling of purpose and glamour. I was a girl from Rockville Centre. Now I was holding Bella's purse while she talked to Representative Carolyn Maloney outside a public hearing, or washing my hands in the bathroom next to Donna Shalala. I even got to call Gloria Steinem and invite her to Bella's birthday party.

But the thrilling moments were laced with anxiety. Small things threw me into a panic. Shirley MacLaine called. She was staying at Bella's that weekend, and did I have a key? (I didn't and felt awful about it.) Beside Bella at the United Nations, I sat with a copy of her remarks in my lap and prayed I had done an adequate job of assembling them. "Where's the speech? These are the wrong pages!" she'd said, glowering, earlier that day. This was standard high-maintenance boss-assistant stuff, but Bella's temper sent me running to the bathroom crying.

I had migraines and stomach cramps. Some of my hair fell out. After three months, I started calling in sick. When getting out of bed became difficult, I went to see a doctor, thinking the problem might be physical. Did I have mono again? My doctor told me to quit. "I've heard stories about Bella," she said.

"I can't quit!" I answered. "I'm going with Bella to the Democratic National Convention. She'll write me a letter of recommendation for graduate school." Working for Bella had made me more ambitious. I wanted to be like the slightly older women in the office who'd studied at Harvard's Kennedy School and traveled to the Conference on Women in Beijing, and who took cabs and ordered Indian food for dinner.

"I suggest you find a therapist who can help you make the transition," the doctor replied.

I picked someone on my insurance plan with a name and address I liked and told her about Bella and, afterward, about my father. Echoing my doctor's advice, the therapist told me I had to quit. From my spot on her couch, I gave my excuses about graduate school and future jobs. From her black leather recliner, she convinced me, in her reassuring and assured way, that I had no choice. She said I was experiencing post-traumatic stress disorder from the childhood abuse, and Bella was my new trigger.

I gave my notice effective immediately, told the unemployment office I was being harassed at work, and went into weekly therapy. In that small hushed office in the Village, with the comforting sound of a noise machine and the view of a brick wall, I began to deal—truly deal—with my past. Not by offering up forgiveness to my parents, or by confronting them in any outward way at all, but by going inside and allowing myself to take in the seriousness and sadness of what had happened to me. It was grueling work. At first I could manage to talk for only a few minutes about my childhood.

But my therapist urged me to search my past and recount specific episodes of abuse rather than hide behind my day-to-day problems. It was necessary to remember in order to eventually start feeling better, she said. Week after week I resisted. Any story I dredged up in her office meant nightmares and headaches and fighting off the desire to slit my wrists for the rest of the week. She persevered. Slowly I began to talk about the violence: My first memory of the pink handprint on my back. The wooden oar smacked across my brother's body. My mother slammed against the refrigerator. The words my father hurled at me. The ways my mother disappointed me with her complicity. My therapist explained that sensitive child or not, rebellious teenager or not, I bore *none* of the responsibility for the violence in my childhood home. No victim of child abuse does.

*　　*　　*

It was summer 1996. I was depressed, but I had unemployment checks and unlimited free time. Franny was doing freelance textile design. Her offhand doodles would eventually end up as designs on plates at Anthropologie or as wallpaper patterns, but she booked jobs only when she was really desperate for cash or saving for a plane ticket back to Mexico. Most of the time she just hung out.

We became inseparable again. We were closest when we were between jobs, when we were depressed, when we were single. She stayed over a lot, sleeping in my bed with me. That summer we lived cheap. We took care of each other. Our friendship was once again daily and emotionally immersive. We ate bagels and falafels, freaking out when we were charged four dollars for the falafel platter rather than the two-fifty for the falafel sandwich advertised in the window on First Avenue. We flirted for late-night drinks at cheap bars. On mornings when I felt sad, she encouraged me to take a shower and a walk. We spent afternoons lying out on frayed beach towels in Tompkins Square Park.

When night came, we'd pre-drink forty-ounce beers with Franny's childhood best friend, Jane, at my place or Jane's on the Lower East Side like we were still in college, then go to Ludlow Lounge or Max Fish or the same old bar on Seventh Street and Avenue B, or else a house party someone had heard about in Chinatown or in an apartment on Avenue D or somewhere in Brooklyn. Or we'd meet up with Vassar people at restaurants and bars we couldn't afford and hope someone with a corporate job or trust fund would buy the drinks and order appetizers for the table. A couple of times Franny and I brought men we'd just met back to my apartment after the bars shut down. One guy came over, ostensibly to play Scrabble. We were all too drunk and tired to finish the game, and halfway through he suggested we go to sleep in my futon bed. But as he and Franny slept, I lay awake that early morning, staring at the knife set I'd inherited from Mark and Abigail, perched menacingly a couple of feet away on the single square foot of kitchen counter. Anything could have happened. After that Franny and I promised: no more strangers.

*　　*　　*

My parents warned me that pretty soon I'd have to quit the city and move home with them if I didn't find a job. A Vassar friend told me about a position coordinating volunteers and volunteer programs at the 14th Street Y, a Jewish community center around the corner from my apartment. The Y was part of the Educational Alliance, a century-old Lower East Side settlement house. I got along so well with the social worker interviewing me, and we talked for such a long time, that we had to stop in the middle of our conversation to take a joint bathroom break. I got the job. The work wasn't glamorous, but it felt solid and meaningful. My boss and I became close. She even found me a more affordable apartment in Williamsburg, Brooklyn (which was still cheap back then).

I placed volunteers in jobs around the agency, from a community center in a housing project to a nursery school near Delancey Street. We ran a service matching volunteers with elderly women and men who needed help getting to the supermarket and to doctors' appointments. We started a tutoring program for high school kids, and a summer reading program for younger children that met in a community garden. Franny, Karen, and Kathy all came and tutored every Thursday night.

Around the time I started my job at the Y, I met David. He was a friend of Jane's roommate. They were part of a tight group of guys from Queens who had all gone to Hunter College High School, an Upper East Side magnet school for gifted kids that was supposed to be one of the best public schools in the country. David was raised in a pricey neighborhood called Jamaica Estates, had gone to Dartmouth, and worked as a programmer for the hedge fund D. E. Shaw. One day he was supposed to take over his father's successful sheet-metal factory in the Bronx. He seemed like the nice Jewish boy my mother had been praying I'd meet. I liked David because he was sarcastic and self-deprecating and well read and good-looking in a bearish sort of way. I tried not to notice that he looked kind of like my brother Josh.

We traveled to Costa Rica and walked through cloud forests and bathed in hot springs by a dormant volcano. In New Hampshire we hiked from hut to hut in the White Mountains and stayed at a cabin in the woods. (We didn't know enough to bring groceries from the city and made do with canned beans and white bread from the closest general store as we swatted off blackflies.) I fasted with his family on Yom Kippur and met them for Sunday dinners at restaurants around the city.

David was generous, always convincing me to let him pay, or at least pay more, since his salary was several times mine. Officially, he lived with roommates in Manhattan, but he usually slept at my railroad apartment in Williamsburg. He said that after we were married, we'd have a brownstone in Brooklyn and a house in the country. I could do whatever I wanted, he promised—nonprofit work or writing. We went to a bedding sale at ABC Carpet, and he bought me a duvet cover and pillowcases. "You deserve nice things," he told me. "Money is more important than you think," he added, sounding like my parents. Instead of being grateful, I turned angry, unable to accept his well-intentioned gift. I exploded. Did he think I was a prostitute? I asked him. Did he not think I could take care of myself?

Soon enough, I grew resentful of David's money and

decided there must be something wrong with him. He wasn't skinny like Ben. He was too negative. He lacked passion about work. On a weekend trip to Vermont, he offhand-edly mentioned wanting to be a sheep farmer, something that seemed perfectly reasonable to me but to David was just something you say while driving through the country. I picked on him for not going after his dreams. (How, ex-actly? Go to sheep-farmer school? Buy a flock?) I needled him for the occasional nights when he went out with friends for things he knew I wouldn't approve of—strip clubs, coke—and about his overbearing mother, who spent her days shopping and seemed nearly as manipulative as my own.

We began fighting, yelling and screaming so loudly that my landlady had to bang on the door to my apartment and tell us to be quiet. I was applying to graduate school in public policy. David said I needed to stay in New York with him, that I couldn't survive graduate school problem sets or loans on my own, and that we couldn't survive a long-distance relationship. I was angry; I cursed him. I pushed him. He held my wrists down tight.

After a year and a half of dating, we broke up. I knew I had to figure myself out—to learn how to behave better and expect more—or else I'd end up in a relationship like my parents'. In the lonely weeks that followed, I quit smoking and found a yoga center where we sang Hindu chants to a harmonium before practicing our poses. But outside the yoga room, I felt empty when I wasn't busy with work or relationship or friend drama. A hipster volunteer in my tutoring program had been flirting with me. When I called and mentioned my breakup with David, he asked me out. I casually made the plan for New Year's Eve so I wouldn't have to be alone that night, and to make David jealous. (We were talking off and on.) The hipster and I went to a Brooklyn loft party and kissed on the sidewalk at midnight. I'd forgotten the heat of beginnings. Back in my bedroom, he tore my underpants off. The next day David called, wanting to see me. We went for cheeseburgers. He hadn't meant the things he'd said, he told me. He'd been an asshole and was sorry. We should get married.

I wasn't ready for that. I needed to see what life was like away from David, away from my family, and away from New York. But even in leaving my family, I needed them. Mark was living in San Francisco, and when I went out to California to visit UC Berkeley, I stayed with him. It felt weird and wrong to be spending time with him after Cincinnati. Nothing had changed in the years since our conversation at Josh's wedding. I wasn't worried about my physical safety, but I definitely didn't feel safe emotionally or okay about our relationship. I stayed with him anyway. I told myself he was still my brother. And it wasn't like I could afford a hotel. I'd flown there on Mark's frequent-flyer miles. We were on our best behavior. We walked around the Mission and took photographs of ourselves in front of the mural art. He took me for good sushi. I tried to act normal. I *wanted* to be able to forgive Mark. I wanted to be someone who could forget and move on.

In the end, I didn't get into Berkeley or Harvard, but I heard back with acceptances from Columbia and the

University of Wisconsin–Madison. Madison offered me a full fellowship. Columbia, where David wanted me to go, would mean getting to stay in New York but taking on serious student-loan debt. And so I gave up my apartment, said goodbye to my friends, and made plans to head to the Midwest.

Franny and Natalie slept over on my last weekend in Brooklyn. Franny read our tarot cards, predicting that everything would work out fine for me, but I wasn't so sure. We held a sidewalk sale of my already secondhand furniture and old clothes. The next day we got up late and went for cheese omelets at the Polish diner that used to be on Bedford Avenue before Williamsburg turned chic. Then my father came to get me.

THIRTEEN

"HOW DARE YOU keep me waiting?"

My father was fuming. He slammed the car door shut behind him, revved the engine, and started screaming at me. I was *fucking ungrateful,* that's what. And I could have been raped. "Who the hell do you think you are?"

He'd been sitting in the parking lot of a suspect potential apartment rental on the outskirts of Madison while I'd gone inside to talk to a would-be roommate, a conversation that had lasted longer than expected. Twenty-six years old, and still my father was yelling and cursing at me. But I'd needed a ride out to Wisconsin, and since I didn't have the money to rent a car, or a friend with a car and a week to spare, I'd relented and agreed to let him take me. The road trip was typical of our relationship. We'd had some unexpectedly and unnervingly good talks, some awkward conversations skirting the difficult contours of our shared history, and plenty of tension-filled silences. At night in a motel room somewhere in the middle of Ohio, I slept fitfully. The sound of his snores from the next bed kept me awake.

I'd arrived in Madison not knowing a soul and with

very little money. After the fight in the parking lot, I missed David and wondered if I'd made a mistake by leaving New York. Still needing a place to live, I went to dinner at a housing cooperative I'd heard about right on the lake. Martha's was a huge, happy, rundown brick house filled with students, self-proclaimed socialist-style "workers," and assorted activists, vegans, dreamers, and single moms. Dirty, contented children ran barefoot while we sat down to a home-cooked vegetarian feast. After dinner, some of the housemates cleaned up, while others relaxed on one of the three painted porches outfitted with swings and hammocks and plants that doubled as ashtrays, or traded shoulder massages in the living room. When my father, who was leaving the next day, stopped by after dinner to pick me up, even he thought the whole scene was great.

Plus, the rent was cheap. For $250 a month and time spent on "work jobs" like child care, cooking, and cleaning, I'd be given room and board: a prepared dinner every night, Sunday brunch, homemade bread, a pantry stocked with dry goods, and a refrigerator busy with eggs, loose tofu, thick slabs of Wisconsin cheese, and local produce. The house had a living room filled with old couches, guitars, and bikes, and a ready-made social life. I showed up for brunch the following morning and arranged an interview for after dinner. A four-person quorum of housemates assembled in a bedroom and asked me, "What do you do to fight racism in your everyday life?" and "Do you have a problem with nudity?"

I moved in, relieved to say goodbye to my father. Martha's became my home. We were ragtag, borrowing each other's clothes, and Dumpster diving. There I found a group of unconventional and independent-minded friends who helped me realize that growing up in a dysfunctional family doesn't mean you have to become a fucked-up adult. Equally eye-opening was that living on several hundred dollars a month—easily managed between my fellowship, cheap grad school habits, a string of research assistant jobs, and a small student loan—meant I was no longer financially dependent on my parents.

Many of my housemates had rougher and much more hardscrabble upbringings than mine, or at least had families with less money. Some came from working-class areas or rural towns. They seemed to be managing fine without the suburban privileges I'd taken for granted. Once my graduate program started, I made friends with other East and West Coast types, but I preferred to spend the weekends with my Martha's friends. I taught free yoga classes in the living room and spent my afternoons studying at a cooperatively run café. I met a guy named Jay, who'd grown up poor and was working his way through his BA; he wore round John Lennon glasses and striped railroad-conductor overalls and didn't talk to his family at all, he said, which both unsettled and impressed me.

*   *   *

A few months after moving into Martha's, I flew back to New York. My Vassar friend Natalie was having a black-tie wedding at the New-York Historical Society. I'd heard the flowers had cost as much as a year's tuition at Vassar. I arrived at Claire's apartment that late-September Saturday afternoon with my dress in a shopping bag. It was a deep pink Nicole Miller gown that the bride had helped me dig up for fifty dollars at a designer discount store before I'd left for Madison. Natalie had asked me to read a passage from the Song of Songs at the ceremony.

Franny seemed different. She wore her black eyeliner heavy and smudged, and she had on a filmy and uncharacteristically dramatic black dress of her mother's with a translucent light green cape over her shoulders. She was very skinny, ten pounds under her normal thin, and was living in a sketchy-sounding apartment in Hell's Kitchen. I must have seemed extraterrestrial, with my talk of econ problem sets, of chocolate peanut butter ice cream cones eaten by the lake, of late-night bike rides and housing co-op kissing parties. Franny and I sat at a table with guys I'd met freshman year. They ignored me, and this time Franny did, too, spending most of the reception outside smoking with them or off in the bathroom.

I went back to Madison, and Franny wouldn't return my calls; I didn't call so much after that. A couple of months after Natalie's wedding, I hitched a ride with some friends who were going to a labor protest in New York, and drove all the way from Madison in a packed car filled with our marijuana smoke. We ended up drinking at Jane's parents' brownstone in Chelsea. The Vassar guys I'd never liked came over, and Jane and Franny huddled in a corner, re-telling old stories about childhood and camp. Another time,

Franny and I sat in the kitchen of her apartment with two bottles of wine and two packs of cigarettes, even though I'd quit, and ordered Chinese takeout. But Franny was distracted all night and wouldn't tell me what was really going on with her, and I left the next morning feeling hurt and lonely.

Never mind her. There was a whole world outside of New York, I told myself. In Madison, I began to slowly change my life. Moving into Martha's allowed me to put more emotional distance between my family and me. In grad school, I slogged through the required classes for my program, economics and statistics, government and social welfare policy, and signed up for some classes that actually interested me—a creative writing workshop, a literature class where we read Harriet Jacobs's *Incidents in the Life of a Slave Girl,* beginning ballet, and a couple of sociology courses on social inequality. At a café on State Street where a fellow co-oper added free extra espresso shots to my lattes, I reunited with a friend from my Nepal trip whom I hadn't seen since Kathmandu. At Martha's we hosted parties where I kissed men, women, and college boys. I babysat a housemate's baby, helped cook dinner and do the dishes for thirty, and harvested vegetables at a community-supported agriculture farm right outside the city. I dated a guy who worked at the revolutionary bookstore; an undergrad who'd hiked the Appalachian Trail; an activist; a history postdoc who criticized my thrift-store clothes. In spring and summer and fall I biked around town. In winter I walked up Bascom Hill and let snowflakes freeze my eyelashes. I smoked a couple of drags of a joint each night before bed to calm my nightmares.

My life tumbled uncontrollably forward. Maybe this was the way my parents had lived their lives, too. I wasn't in therapy anymore; I'd given that up when I left New York.

My father called and offered me a reliable extra car that had been my grandmother's before they moved her to a nursing home. I took it, rationalizing that I needed the car to drive to Iowa, where I was planning to spend the summer working in a Des Moines housing project for the I Have a Dream Foundation. I was conducting a participatory program evaluation, which meant doing a lot of interviews. With my clipboard and questions, I sat in orderly kitchens, was welcomed into TV-blaring living rooms, and hung out on sticky-hot midsummer stoops. In the evenings I read on a porch swing or went for bike rides. One Saturday night I went on a date with an Iowa City artist I'd met back in New York who drove two hours to see me. We got burgers and beer and spent a magic hour waiting out a thunderstorm in the backseat of my car.

*   *   *

In the middle of the summer I left Iowa for a week. Mark was getting married at the Tower of David in Jerusalem. (How else to top the Waldorf?) Tamara was a tough, sexy woman with olive skin and a pixie haircut. She'd grown up mostly in Australia, but her parents now lived in a ritzy suburb of Tel Aviv. My parents said I had to fly in for the wedding. They bought my plane ticket and booked me a room at their hotel.

I took my assigned place under the chuppah with the rest of the two families as Tamara circled Mark the requisite seven times. My new silky black dress grazed my ankles. Swept up in the evening, I kissed my brother on the cheek after he broke the glass. But I'd never forgiven Mark for hurting me. After the reception, I came down with a fever.

Before school started up again, I flew to San Francisco for Mark and Tamara's California wedding party at a Napa Valley vineyard. I had on another new dress my mother had bought me, this one long and flowered. Monica, my girlhood friend from Rockville Centre, was living in San Francisco, and this time I slept over at her place. We showed up to the party high and late. I hated being there, hated having to smile and look pretty and sound intelligent and fake my relationship with my brother, especially among his Stanford MBA friends. These people respected and admired Mark, as I once had. One couple had flown in all the way from Japan to be there. What would happen if they knew the truth? If they'd seen him slam me against the bathroom wall? That weekend a knotty lump on the back of my neck grew inflamed, making me jittery with pain.

On the plane ride home to Madison, the pain kept getting worse. I swallowed too many Tylenols and Advils, ordered a drink, and looked forward to the joint waiting for me at Martha's. But over the next few days, I couldn't keep up with the sharp ache and went to see a doctor and then a specialist. He said I'd developed a cyst inside my throat and another at the back of my neck. The specialist removed them both that day, even though I'd come to the appointment alone and driven myself. They were benign but could recur, he said, handing me a prescription for painkillers. I wanted to know what had caused the growths. My Madison yoga teacher wondered if something metaphorical was stuck in the back of my throat. Words? Was there anything I needed to say that I hadn't let myself? The specialist, on the other hand, said it was probably HPV, perhaps something I'd picked up when giving a blow job.

*   *   *

Then, in a sociology seminar on social change, I spotted Neil. Legs crossed, glasses and goatee, hiking boots and flannel shirt, tattered paperback of whatever ethnography we were reading that week, discussing the Chicago School, whatever that was, with quiet confidence. He was auditing the class and showed up when he felt like it. Neil was "promising," which in his case meant he'd already had articles published in some of the best sociology journals and been summoned to give a job talk at the University of Chicago. I paid attention, but only a little.

After the class ended, Neil emailed and asked me out for coffee. We spoke on the phone to make arrangements. I loved his voice and made note of the calm, careful way he listened when I spoke, and how good I felt after talking to him. Not manic and elated but grounded and appreciated. This was something new. I was interested. Very interested. I borrowed a housemate's jeans and put on a fitted purple shirt I splurged on at Urban Outfitters, along with the well-made black cloth coat Natalie had advised me to buy on sale before leaving New York.

Neil and I met at the cooperative café (because he had asked where I liked to hang out). It was snowing, and what did I think about taking our coffees to go and going sledding? We traded turns riding our makeshift sled—the plastic rectangle meant to go underneath a dish rack—down a snowy hill. Afterward we went for wine and pizza. Neil's car had a busted heater and a rusted-out hole on the floor of the passenger seat, covered by newspapers and books, but our conversation kept me warm. Over the next few weeks we would go ice-skating on a pond, dance to eighties music at a cheesy club in town, and hear a piano concert at the university's Music Hall. We sat in neighborhood bars, drinking Wisconsin beer. For Valentine's Day, I gave him my copy of Wallace Stegner's *Crossing to Safety*. We stayed up all night, kissing and falling in love. I started daydreaming about a life with him.

Neil was different. For starters, he was from California. Not like the hipster Vassar and New York City boys I'd dated, with their studied cool, nor the earnest hippie Madison activists, he was academic and ambitious. This was a combination I hadn't encountered often. There was something else. Neil, in a youthful act of ironic rebellion from his parents, had worked as a police officer between college and graduate school. Though he must have been the gentlest cop on the street, I took comfort in knowing he could protect me.

When I stayed over at Neil's apartment, a grown-up place with central air, a stocked fridge, and books stacked on a dusty weight-training bench, he cooked for me and happily handed over the front section of the newspaper. He was brilliant and handsome and going places, yes, but also a nonconformist with zero tolerance for bad behavior—including mine—and the sort of emotional manipulations I was used to. When he heard me on the phone with my parents, Neil looked uneasy. He didn't like the way we talked to one another or the way I tore myself apart afterward, and he seemed to understand why I sometimes vigilantly avoided their calls.

Neil was an only child with parents who'd moved from Los Angeles to Northern California, one town over from Berkeley. His father, Herb, was an aspiring novelist who'd practiced entertainment law before heading north and settling down to a career as an editor for a university legal publishing company. He read constantly, from philosophy to psychoanalysis to poetry.

Neil's mother, Sonya (nicknamed Sunny for her disposition), had left college at nineteen to get married and put her husband through law school with an office job at Frederick's of Hollywood. Later on, she became a creatively inclined (if somewhat frustrated) stay-at-home mom who took a young Neil to school and camp and the petting zoo in Tilden Park, and threw dinner parties for her gourmet club, cooking from Julia Child's cookbook.

Sonya and Herb were Jewish but steadfastly secular. They were intellectuals and atheists and armchair Marxists who put up Christmas trees and lit Menorahs, who organized Easter-egg hunts and served latkes and pastrami sandwiches. They lived quietly and contentedly as three. Like my parents, they'd made it to Europe as a family only once, but with hardcovers and paperbacks purchased at Moe's and Cody's and Black Oak and University Press Books crowding their small house, stacks upon stacks of them, they were far more worldly than my parents.

Years before we met, when she was fifty-seven and Neil was just a college student, Sonya became sick with a fast-moving cancer. She died at home later that year. When Neil left California for graduate school, he called his father every day. They were best friends.

Neil didn't care about being cool, something I'd worked on diligently since ninth grade. He loved his studies and put them before anything else. Out for Sunday breakfast one freezing morning six weeks into our relationship, I suggested we take the newspaper and get back into bed for the day. Neil turned cold. The thought horrified him. He had *work* to do.

I felt rejected, and I felt like an idiot for wasting my twenties pursuing men. Why had I signed up for a degree in a subject I was no more than vaguely interested in? Why hadn't I tried to do something I loved? It was too late, I figured. Instead I'd focus on our future. Aloud. I pushed, was always pushing. I was impatient; I wanted to know how this would end up. I wanted us to be together forever.

Inevitably, Neil asked for space. I protested weakly. We went to separate parties that Saturday night. I kissed someone else, a co-op guy, maybe the revolutionary bookseller. On a final late-night phone call, after I begged him to come over to discuss the end of our relationship in person, Neil refused, and I gave up.

"I love you," I said right before we hung up. "I thought you should know."

I hadn't said this before. The next day Neil flew home to see his father in California.

*　　*　　*

About a week later, Neil called. His father, Herb, had had a heart attack. They'd eaten lunch at a Thai restaurant and then come home, Neil napping on the couch; Herb working on a short story in front of the computer; the rest a secondhand blur. Neil performing CPR. The EMTs' attempt to restart Herb's heart. The ambulance ride. Herb, seventy-one, brought to the same Berkeley hospital where Neil was born twenty-eight years earlier. Nothing could be done.

He didn't want me to fly out for the funeral. But he did want to talk. I made him promise to call me the next day, and again the next, and then the next one after that.

After the funeral I picked Neil up at the Madison airport. He was standing by the baggage carousel, looking solemn and older and utterly alone. He was the only one left in his family.

We went back to his apartment and sat down on the living room couch. He started to cry, waves of exhaustion and tears, an onslaught. I held him. The days and weeks continued on like that. Neil wearing his black bathrobe and flannel pajamas all day, until one day he decided to get dressed. We saw a movie with his friends, *Boys Don't Cry*. We went for Indian food. We fell into bed and started over.

For the first time in my relationship history, I had to be the strong one and not worry about whether we'd end up together. I didn't press him about the future. I was applying for jobs in New York for after graduation, and Neil had no idea where he'd be teaching after he finished his Ph.D. I tried to appreciate the time we had together without thinking ahead.

Neil met my parents when they came to Madison for my graduation that May. The four of us drove out for a house tour of Frank Lloyd Wright's Taliesin. There must have been a celebratory graduation meal, but I can't remember any details. Perhaps Neil sat with them during the ceremony. As difficult as my relationship with my parents was, I wanted Neil to like them.

That late spring or early summer, Neil and I took a trip to the Bay Area to pack up his parents' house. Herb had left behind a huge personal library of fiction and history and sociology and philosophy and religion. It would take a lifetime to read all those books, Neil said, so he wanted none of them, and he impulsively sold the collection to a Berkeley bookstore. Sunny's rings and necklaces sat in her jewelry box, though she had died a decade before. He threw out some tangled costume stuff, and wrapped an antique engagement ring and wedding band in tissue paper, tucking them in the front pocket of his jeans.

We returned to California later in the summer, this time to Palo Alto. Mark and Tamara had a new baby, and my parents sent a ticket, instructing me to come for the bris, the circumcision. Neil joined me on the trip and sat at breakfast and dinner tables, looking uncomfortable. My father and brothers congratulated him on the car he'd bought with money from the sale of his father's house. At dinner, my mother chastised Tamara for eating sushi while breast-feeding, and Tamara walked out of the restaurant. My family—all of us, including me—were critical, argumentative, and bossy.

In Madison, I packed up my room at Martha's and came upon the plainly written paperback *Outgrowing the Pain*, which I read with renewed conviction. In particular, I noticed a sentence I'd underlined furiously in college but was just now ready to believe: *For whatever reason, whether you were neglected or abused physically, sexually, or emotionally, it was a problem with your parents, not with you.*

FOURTEEN

ON AN AUGUST Sunday morning, I woke up in my child-hood bedroom on Long Island, not knowing my life was about to change. I was just in from Madison and back in my parents' house before a week of job interviews in the city.

I'd been gone and back for years, gone and back since as early as I could leave—to those theater summer programs and then to college, to Nepal and then to Israel, to my beloved crappy apartments in the East Village and Brooklyn, and then to graduate school. But somehow, as far as I ventured, I always found myself back here in this bedroom.

My room was exactly the same. The Laura Ashley wallpaper my mother and I had picked out together, the matching white bed and dresser and schoolgirl desk. The stereo handed down from Mark and Josh, and an old TV sitting on a wood cabinet that one of them had made in a high school industrial arts class. Posters from school plays hung on the back of the door next to pictures of J. Crew models cut out from the catalog, scruffy guys with intense eyes in roll-neck sweaters. My menagerie of stuffed animals on wicker shelving. Buried somewhere deep inside my closet was a Raggedy Ann doll and her mate, Andy.

The door still had the skeleton lock my father had installed when I'd hit puberty. Sleeping there for the first time in several months, I'd made sure to lock myself in before bed.

Perhaps this visit would consist of nothing more than sushi in town, strip-mall Italian food, and a trip to the Roosevelt Field mall for an interview outfit. I was older now, an adult. I had Neil back in Madison and five job interviews in Manhattan scheduled for the coming week.

I got out of bed, visited the retro bathroom I used to share with my brothers, and wandered downstairs to make myself breakfast.

My parents had recently renovated their kitchen, hiring professionals rather than having my father take on a DIY project like he used to when we were little, stripping and sanding cabinets over months of weekends. They were proud of the new kitchen. They'd taken out a second mortgage, I think, worked with an interior designer or architect of some sort. Or maybe they'd simply hired a contractor or handyman, but even that sounded to me like something rich people did. It was the sort of kitchen meant to impress the other teachers in my mother's book club, with a cooktop built right in to the requisite granite countertops, a large eat-in island in the shape of a kidney bean, aluminum navy chairs, and stainless-steel appliances. I missed the old kitchen of my childhood with the regular wood table and the clunky yellow fridge. I took a pre-sliced sesame bagel from the stainless-steel freezer and stuck it in the stainless-steel toaster oven.

My father was already downstairs. He was wearing his old green terry-cloth robe over a white Hanes V-neck undershirt and drawstring pajama bottoms worn soft, with a pair of thin slippers on his feet. I'd seen him in some version of these same bedclothes for my entire life. He was fifty-seven, and he and my mother (with her good skin) prided themselves on looking young for their age without any special effort, but his gray hair was coarse and dull, and his pasty skin was rough.

He was in a bad mood. He commandeered the kitchen, huffily and noisily pouring coffee and a second bowl of cereal for himself, acting all of a sudden put out by my very presence. I remembered this feeling viscerally, the feeling of being unwelcome in my own home. Almost always it took me by surprise, hitting just when I'd let myself get comfortable and vulnerable.

I didn't want any trouble. Certainly I didn't want to get into it with him that morning. He liked to blame me for his moods, but this time, at least, I hadn't done anything to deserve his attitude. But then, when I reached for a coffee mug, I miscalculated the weight of a cabinet door and it swung wide open, imperceptibly nicking the new refrigerator. Or had it been the other way around? Had I been reaching for something from the refrigerator and scratched the cabinet?

However it happened, my father was steaming, fuming, the red spots on his face turning textured and pronounced. Like some sort of twisted comic-book character. "You have no idea how much things cost," he said. "Do you know how much I paid for this refrigerator? For this entire kitchen? Do you?"

The tears came immediately. My heart was pounding.

But you could scarcely see the damage, I pointed out. It was an accident. A mistake. I felt horrible and guilty and frightened and in an escalating panic, because I knew I couldn't fix it or repay him. On the other hand, the smudge might be the kind to come off with some sudsy warm water and a paper towel.

It was a small thing, a petty thing. But I knew that in their house small things could have consequences.

My father slammed cabinets, rattling canned goods. *Did I even respect his things? Did I even respect him?*

So this was what it was going to be like. Still.

I tried to calm myself down. I took my coffee into the family room where my parents kept the computer. I needed to print out hard copies of my résumé in case my interviewers asked for them. I wanted everything to be just so, to be perfect. What I wore and my résumé and the answers I'd give to questions like "Tell me one of your weaknesses" and the way I'd charm and convince myself into a do-gooder nonprofit job paying forty-five thousand a year—an unimaginable sum to me at the time—and, if I was lucky, an apartment in brownstone Brooklyn.

Plus, I thought changing rooms might diffuse the argument.

I sat down at my father's desk and tried to figure out the uncooperative printer.

They'd bought a new carpet and a matching plaid overstuffed couch and love seat for the family room, but the walls were lined with the same fake wood paneling from when we'd moved in twenty years before, and the shelves were still stuffed with my brothers' sports trophies, my horseback-riding camp participation ribbons and drama club plaques, and the small handprints on gray ceramic slabs that we'd made as preschoolers.

"Get up," he said, coming into the room. "Stand right there," he ordered, pointing to his right. He wanted me to watch while he sat and worked the printer. He was telling me that, even now, I couldn't get a job without his help, without his goddamn shitty printer.

We'd had thousands of these fights before. Fights that started out stupid and petty and meaningless but escalated until he scared me to death. We fought in person when we were together, and when I moved away, we fought in letters and over the phone. In Madison I'd held the phone to Neil's ear so he could hear my father scream at me, like I used to do with Franny.

But that day, for some unknown reason, I felt something new stirring. Was it courage? Was it no longer giving a shit? Was it the knowledge that I could go to Kinko's? All I knew was I couldn't, *I wouldn't,* slink away again, wouldn't run to my room and hide.

"Don't you talk to me that way," I said. I was so done, so sick of him trying to intimidate and threaten me. "Don't you *ever* speak to me like that again." I would not put up with his bullshit for one more minute.

I can't remember his exact words back. Maybe he said "Who do you think you are." Maybe he called me a bitch or a cunt. Eventually he grew strangely quiet in the face of my long-pent-up wrath. That morning I wouldn't be stopped. I went further, confronting him with his behavior, my wording harsher and blunter than it had ever been in my therapist-approved, cautiously phrased letters of reconciliation and obligatory, compulsory forgiveness. It was time. I needed him to understand *exactly* what he'd done to me. And I wanted him to admit it.

My mother was sitting on the couch, laying low and pretending to read the Sunday paper.

"You hit me. You hit Josh and Mark," I said to him. "And you hit her, too," I added, turning to my mother.

Now I really had gone too far. My mother couldn't avoid the confrontation any longer.

"How many times did I hit you? How many?" he demanded, his voice exploding. I wasn't sure if he was talking to her or to me.

"Too many to count," she answered. Her words sliced the room in two. I'd never heard her stand up to him like this before. I'd never seen her take my side.

My father fixed his eyes on me. "You were a difficult child," he said. "You were stubborn. Sensitive. Selfish. You were a brat. You always knew how to push my buttons. It was both of our faults. You and me, we were both to blame."

"I was a *child,*" I begged him to see. "It was not my fault." It had taken me my entire life to understand that.

"Jessie's right," my mother said, an admission I'd forever longed to hear. "She was two and a half the first time you hit her."

Two and a half years old? I didn't know that. I asked

my mother to tell me the story, and a part of me wanted to crawl into her lap to hear it. But she wasn't that kind of mother. And I suppose I wasn't that sort of daughter, either.

"We were heading out on a neighborhood walk," she said. I'd insisted that we leave the stroller at home. I wanted to walk the whole way myself and promised I could make it. Halfway to wherever we were going, I changed my mind and cried myself into a tantrum, begging to be carried. That was when he'd hit me. That was the first time.

How could he hit a *toddler*? How could anyone?

"Why didn't you protect me?" I asked my mother. "When it kept happening, why didn't you leave? You had a job. You make almost as much money as he does."

She had three young children. "And I would have lost the house," she said. "We would have had to move into an apartment in town."

I pictured the small apartment in the middle of Rockville Centre where a classmate of mine had lived with his mother after her divorce. How I'd envied him that apartment. I'd *wanted* my mother to leave, to divorce him. Didn't she get that? I'd wanted her to take my side.

"Would that have been so bad?" I said. "We would have been safe."

*   *   *

Our conversation continued into the late morning and early afternoon, hour after hour of the three of us in the family room, crying and accusing.

I wanted them to understand how the abuse had changed me. How I had nightmares. How I woke up sweating and screaming. How lost I'd been feeling. How alone and rudderless. How I wanted a family, but not this kind. There had to be a way to make them understand that there was no excuse for hurting a child, for having hurt me. I needed them to take responsibility.

But they hedged and defended and blamed and made excuses.

After a while the three of us started to lose our voices.

"I should have gotten a divorce," my mother eventually admitted, sighing her saddest, most exhausted sigh. Finally.

Perhaps she still could leave? she suggested. Maybe she could come live with me?

I tried to imagine sharing an apartment in the city with her now. We could take care of each other like I'd hoped we would back when my father and brothers went to Boy Scout camp. Did I owe her that? Then I came to my senses. *No.* I was a grown woman and finally free. Besides, she *wanted* to be with him. We all knew there was no longer any point in her leaving him for my sake.

Fuck. My interviews. I called my college friend Natalie. Broken and shaky from the day, I asked if I could please stay with her. She and her husband were splitting up, and she'd very recently kicked him out, but she invited me to spend the week anyway.

*   *   *

I hadn't planned on never speaking to my parents again, not when I stupidly agreed to let them drive me to Natalie's apartment in Manhattan rather than take the train with my suitcase. Not when we got stuck in Sunday-night back-from-the-Hamptons traffic, me crying in the backseat, with R.E.M.'s "Don't Go Back to Rockville" blasting on my head-phones like a teenager. Not when I hugged them goodbye outside the car and told them that I loved them.

Not even right after that, when we realized my mother had accidentally locked the keys in the car and my father screamed for me to *get him some goddamn wire hangers*. And when, instead of staying to help them, I ran into Natalie's building.

Natalie had a father in real estate, a job at a magazine, and a loft apartment in the Flatiron District with a gourmet kitchen and his-and-hers bathrooms. Her wedding had been featured in a bridal magazine.

"Lock the door," I directed when she let me in. Her apartment was better than the one on *Friends*. She was giving me a tour when my father started buzzing her doorbell.

"Don't answer that," I pleaded. "Please!" Natalie backed away from the intercom, startled. She hadn't realized my father was *this* crazy. Should we maybe call the police?

We moved to the far end of the apartment, where an enormous wall was lined with windows, and watched the action on the street below like it was a movie of someone else's life.

My father had found some sort of a crowbar and shattered the driver's-side window of his Subaru so that he wouldn't have to prolong that horrible day for one minute more. The broken glass on the street looked oddly beautiful against the asphalt, like shards of diamond.

"Don't call me" was what I'd said to my parents back when we were standing on the street saying goodbye. We had yelled and screamed and cried, and I had confronted him. But we'd done those things, to one degree or another, many times before. At least he hadn't hit me. And my mother had taken my side. That was something. Progress, it felt like. I'd give myself a week. Maybe two. A breather. I wanted space, perspective. I needed to get through my job interviews.

That night I couldn't stop crying. Would my father come back for me? I felt frail and frightened and unsafe. How would I make it in the world without them? I had no money, no job, and I had moved out of Martha's to spend the summer with Neil. We were in love, but the relationship was very new, and we'd already broken up once.

Natalie filled the bathtub, lit an aromatherapy candle, and ordered takeout. She had a doorman, she reminded me. We'd be fine. Maybe she gave me something to help me sleep. Eventually I did.

I saw my mother the next morning. A coda on a street corner in Manhattan, a detail of the story I like to push away. Earlier that weekend my parents had taken me clothes shopping and bought me two interview outfits: a long skirt and matching top at Ann Taylor, and a black petite Tahari pantsuit that was on sale at a mall department store. The suit fit fine, but the Ann Taylor skirt needed hemming. It was at the tailor in Rockville Centre, which was closed on

Sundays. My mother called early Monday morning and said she would bring me the skirt. No matter what had happened between us, she still worried about my looking nice for my interviews. She still loved me.

We met on lower Fifth Avenue. My mother hadn't found a proper parking space and didn't turn the engine off. The skirt, wrapped in dry cleaner's plastic, hung on a hook in the backseat of her car. She was a hoarse mess; so was I. Anxious and angry, I less than halfheartedly thanked her for coming. Part of me was grateful. Part of me hated her.

"You'd better call your father," she said.

I took the parcel and slammed the car door shut.

I never saw either of my parents again.

FIFTEEN

AFTER MY INTERVIEWS, I flew back to Madison to pack my stuff and sell my (their) car, my one source of cash. *See?* I could hear my parents saying, *Money does matter*. I'd spent the summer after graduation living at Neil's while I applied for jobs. He was writing his dissertation with plans to teach there in the fall, but had no idea where he'd end up once he got a tenure-track job, and we hadn't discussed the idea of my waiting around to find out. But now everything had changed. The idea of my moving to New York by myself, given my current state, was ludicrous. I was an inconsolable wreck. I wanted to scratch my insides out, wanted to die, wanted to take a knife and slice open my wrists and lie in a bath and watch myself submerge in lukewarm blood just like I used to fantasize about as a girl. Sunlight hurt my eyes, and I refused to go outside into the August heat. But inside the apartment, I couldn't stop shivering. I begged Neil to check me into a psychiatric institution. I dreamed of sturdy, starched white sheets and a smoking lounge. Something out of *Girl, Interrupted*. Neil suggested I phone my old therapist. It was late August—I was lucky she was around to return my call. We talked over the hum of Neil's central air. I decided not to see or speak to my parents, at least not for the time being.

They were devastated. We had been close, if in a dysfunctional, totally screwed-up sort of way. But we were family, and there was all that history. My mother teaching me how to read while I was in nursery school, my father buying me ballet slippers and winter coats. Now, out of nowhere, it seemed, I'd abandoned them. My mother kept calling. When I was still at Natalie's, it was several times a day, then every few days. For weeks, when I was back in Madison, she left me pleading phone messages. "Call home, come home." Come to your senses. A message from her sent me to bed, made me doubt everything, made my skin crawl.

I let the answering machine pick up. Her voice was still hoarse and gravelly, so I could only imagine what things were like back home. She sounded desperate, which alarmed me. But I was also angry that she seemed more shaken, and had more of a sense of urgency, about our break than she'd ever had about the abuse. I knew I couldn't take on her grief and sorrow and rage. After a month or two, the calls stopped. In their place, a muddy stream of gut-wrenching cards and letters came in the mail. Could I forgive her? Could I be reasonable? She was suicidal, she said—not knowing that I was, too. I'd done that to her. I didn't return her calls.

My father didn't call. Eventually he sent a letter of his own. He was sorry. He loved me and realized that he had a bad temper problem, reminding me that his own father had hit him and admitting that he'd repeated those mistakes.

But he wished I could see that we were *both* to blame. I had been a difficult child. I'd gotten under his skin and made things worse. Even so, he loved me. He wanted to see me. His hurt was plain. I was his favorite, didn't I realize?

I was their daughter. To not have me in their life, to have me excise them from mine, was unnatural, unthinkable. My mother couldn't bear to go on. I'd inflicted a double sentence: the private, immeasurably painful loss of their daughter, and then the public humiliation caused by my absence. (What would my mother tell her teacher friends?) I felt ashamed and very guilty, but a part of me took satisfaction in this act of vengeance, in having the upper hand at last. I couldn't change them, or make them sorry enough, but I could punish them with my silence. I could forgive, yes. For my own psychological well-being, I had to, but from a distance. I wrote and explained that I was continuing to process and come to terms with all of it—our relationship, my childhood. I said that I forgave my father, that if they could take full responsibility, then maybe one day we could reconcile.

Neil drove me to New York, where I'd been offered a job at NYU. Neil decided to give up his apartment in Madison and move in with me. He'd fly back and forth, staying on a friend's couch while he taught in Wisconsin that semester. It was a financially preposterous plan and completely un-realistic when it came to the academic job market, but we were in love. And I needed him.

Josh was the only person left in my family I was on speak-ing terms with. Which was strange, because he was the one

I'd been the least close to growing up. He and Rachel had moved to Westchester with their young daughter. We'd never had much in common; he'd embraced the suburban lifestyle of our youth, while I'd automatically rejected anything that struck me as mainstream. But we were family. And Josh had never hit me. He was also a social, friendly, and generally good-natured guy, a natural salesman who wanted people to get along. More than anything, he wanted to have a normal, close all-American family. He set out to be the peacemaker, to smooth things over, to revise the collective memory of our childhoods. From where he stood, *no matter what,* I had to start talking to our parents again. I *had* to reunite the family. He asked me to *please* stop talking about the abuse, to call my parents and make up. I was making everyone's lives impossible, he explained. He seemed embarrassed. He seemed humiliated, even. As for the abuse? It wasn't that bad, he tried to convince me. Forget about it.

One weekend that fall, Josh and Rachel drove to Brooklyn to see me. Neil was in Madison, finishing up there before he'd start teaching a class at Barnard in January. When Josh and Rachel walked into our floor-through one-bedroom apartment in a brownstone with the farmhouse table from Pottery Barn and the new overstuffed couch heaped with colorful pillows, they started questioning my relationship with Neil. We'd bought the furniture with money from the sale of his parents' house. Rachel and Josh disapproved of our living together without being engaged—Neil paying half the rent, for the new furniture, all of it. Rachel wondered aloud how a Wisconsin graduate student could possibly afford (or need) an apartment in Park Slope. "What are you going to do when you break up?" Rachel asked. Given my dating history, it was a good question. I didn't know how to explain that Neil was different, that I was different, too, and that we wouldn't be breaking up.

The last time we saw one another was at their house. I'd brought Neil with me this time. Josh left the game playing on the television in the family room. Rachel was in and out, wearing furry house slippers and sweatpants, looking softer than I'd seen her. Their daughter crawled around a play area. I'd wanted to see my niece and try to keep these last relationships going. But I was so nervous and on edge, being there, that I was trembling. I must have made Josh and Rachel tense, too.

I knew I wasn't strong enough to endure more visits like that. He stopped calling me or I stopped returning his calls. I don't remember my last conversation with my brother. Maybe it was that afternoon in his driveway, Josh giving us directions back to the highway.

*   *   *

In the weeks and months that followed, I tried to tell myself I was doing the right thing by not calling or seeing my parents, but I was more of a wreck than ever, filled with guilt and shame for making the break. Neil felt certain about my decision, and Kathy thought I was doing the right thing, but not many of my other friends understood. Not right away. Would I go back to an abusive husband? I asked myself. No, of course not. But the guilt surrounded me like a shroud.

Who are we without a family? Who was I? What was I supposed to do every year on Thanksgiving? On my birthday? On their birthdays? Would I fast on Yom Kippur and make a seder on Passover? Maybe those parts of my life were over, too. Did I still care about being successful? Or thin and pretty? Or about any of the things my mother had taught me were important? Despite all the bad memories made there, I couldn't believe I'd never again see the inside of my childhood home, have even five minutes to gather keepsakes from my bedroom. There would be no more newspaper clippings sent from my father or shopping trips with my mother. It was as if my entire family had died. What was I supposed to do when I *missed* them?

With Neil in New York, our apartment in Brooklyn, and my job as a public policy researcher at NYU, I had just what I'd hoped for. But I couldn't appreciate my new life. Without a family, it felt like I had nothing. It became harder and harder simply to get out of bed in the mornings. I wasted workdays on the Internet, reading about yoga teacher trainings and meditation retreats, looking for an escape. The only time I felt halfway good about myself, the only time I felt alive, was during yoga class. But afterward I stuffed myself with cheesy pasta or greasy takeout that I couldn't even taste. By the end of that winter, I'd gained twenty-five pounds. I hated my mother and father, but I hated myself, too. Not talking to my parents was in some ways more painful than talking to them. I wondered if I was a horrible, immoral person, a monster, even, for not giving in. It didn't escape me that I'd discovered the courage to walk away from them now that I was in love with a man who'd promised to take care of me. Was I the Jewish-American princess they'd always said I was? Clearly, I was a bad daughter. Maybe I was a bad person, too.

I read that psychiatric patients who enter treatment often get worse before they get better. Several months in, I quit my NYU job. My boss, a high-powered dean who had handpicked and trained me, was livid and told me I had a problem with authority (which of course I did). She came from city government and had connections with nonprofits throughout the city. She said I would never work in New York again. I didn't care. I was relieved to be able to stay in bed. Each new round of depression felt deeper, the effects cumulative. Meanwhile, we were burning through Neil's parents' house money. I drank and ate takeout and cried all day and contemplated ways to commit suicide. I knew I had to leave New York and go someplace cheap where I could get better.

*   *   *

Slowly, over the accumulating no-parent days and weeks and months that followed, something in me switched, clicked. My parents had contaminated the first half of my life. I couldn't let them ruin the second. Even through the fog of my depression, I'd seen glimpses of the person I could perhaps become without them. I couldn't keep accepting their craziness. Not all at once, but as time passed, I stopped feeling guilty.

For my twenty-ninth birthday that May, my mother wrote me a last long letter, sending it along with a sterling-silver charm bracelet in a blue Tiffany box. The bracelet held a bean, a circle, a teardrop, a starfish, and a heart. I knew this was meant to say how much she wished things had been different. I tried it on, simultaneously saddened and moved. Though I understood her intentions, the gift left me feeling empty and misunderstood. I forced myself to read her letter. I could tell how hard she'd worked on crafting it and how many times she'd discussed the wording with her therapist. I imagined her copying down the final version from a second or third draft onto the cream stationery with her name engraved on top. She'd written *To My Beloved Daughter* on the envelope. In swirls of cursive, she talked of insight. She was sorry, in her way. She said she'd failed me. She admitted her lack of courage.

Why couldn't I forgive her? What more did I want her to say? Maybe it didn't matter what she said. It was too late. I put the letter aside; I didn't believe a word. After wearing the bracelet once to the corner coffee place, and being told by the barista how much it cost—hundreds of dollars, by far the most expensive present my mother had ever given me—I stowed it in the back of my underwear drawer and never put it on again.

* * *

Spring was usually my favorite season in New York, but that year I could hardly get myself outside. Around that time, I got a phone call.

"Jessica? It's Ellen."

Ellen was a rabbi, a feminist, and a progressive activist with a congregation in Park Slope, Brooklyn. We'd worked together years before at the 14th Street Y, and I'd admired and looked up to her. Neil and I had gone to her synagogue for High Holy Day services that year, sitting among the hundreds there for the annual rite. On Yom Kippur, tears had run down my face as I'd recounted my sins. I wondered why she was getting in touch.

"This is awkward," she said. "I hope you don't mind my calling like this. But your mother—"

Oh.

"Your mother," she continued, "called me, very upset. I don't want to get in the middle, to go where it's not my place, but she asked me if I could reach out to you. She said you haven't spoken in months."

I collapsed in tears. Eventually, after a few minutes of sobbing into the receiver, I mumbled something about my father and the abuse and that I really was okay now, that this was the best thing.

I ran into the rabbi some weeks later at an ATM on Seventh Avenue, near Key Food. I tried to be brighter, more cheerful. I didn't want her stressing out about me. I wanted to seem like I had it together.

"How are you?" I said, accepting a hug, and then letting myself break down.

*　　*　　*

My mother had dreamed of, and worried over, my getting married since I was a girl. Would I find the right man?

Would he be smart and kind and a go-getter? And Jewish? And what would we do for the wedding? I knew she'd have wanted to be there for each ritual, from engagement party to dress shopping to bridal shower to wedding day. My father would have cried, walking me down the aisle. (How ironic that my parents would have thoroughly approved of Neil, though he wouldn't have been able to stand them.)

One night in our Brooklyn apartment, in the midst of my depression, when I felt like I had nothing to give him, Neil made our favorite spaghetti dinner and asked me to marry him, hiding the ring in a cheese grater. Neil was undeniably good. He was as kind as he was smart. Kinder. I loved him. And I knew this was what I wanted, a life together. We kissed and cried, with wonder about all that was to come. I felt a little less sad and a little more hopeful. But I couldn't even call my parents to tell them we were engaged. And I hadn't been in touch with Franny for a year or two. The next day I sat alone on our stoop and admired the ring in the morning light.

SIXTEEN

NEIL APPLIED FOR jobs and accepted a one-year teaching position at Williams College. The country sounded good, like a psychiatric institution—lite. I was worn out and couldn't function in Brooklyn anymore, emotionally or financially.

We rented a carriage house in a small town in upstate New York, over a mountain pass and across the state line from Williamstown, Massachusetts. There we could have an entire house for half of what we'd been paying for a one-bedroom in Park Slope.

Once a week I held a children's story time at the library down the road. As the weather turned colder, we warmed ourselves with homemade chili and piles of books. In the mornings I started writing, and in the afternoons and evenings I taught yoga around town. The trunk of my station wagon loaded with mats and blankets and foam blocks, I taught at the college, and in pay-what-you-wish classes in drafty community centers, and subbed at a ritzy Berkshires spa. Neil taught and finished his dissertation. He began receiving invitations to campuses across the country

239

to give talks at sociology departments looking to hire assistant professors for the following year. We planned a tiny late-spring wedding. But depression and anxiety held me tight in their grip.

*   *   *

Then, on a quiet and solitary November weekend, when Neil was flying home from a job interview in California, the phone rang. I ignored it. I didn't know anyone for a hundred miles. Voice mail picked up.

My father.

"I'm in Williamstown. I'd like to meet for coffee." He told me he was staying at the 1896 Motel and left a room number.

I was taken aback by his voice, the reality of it. This was the precise scenario that made me drench my bedsheets with sweat at four in the morning—me alone, my father coming for me.

"I need to see you."

How had he tracked me down? And why, for God's sake, had I stupidly suggested we live in this remote rural town rather than near the college?

"We need to talk."

I panicked. My pulse raced, my body suddenly on high alert. Neil was on a plane, unreachable for hours. The view out my study window of quiet woods turned dangerous and foreboding. Maybe it was the still-unfamiliar rural setting, or the all-too-familiar sound of his voice, or my depression.

Maybe I was having a PTSD reaction, but I felt sure I was in mortal danger.

This time, I thought, *my father is going to kill me.*

I imagined my father with a knife. A gun. Or even his bare hands. How humiliated he must be for what I'd done to him and how I'd ruined our family. How he'd make me pay.

I called Kathy. She'd been there for me since seventh grade. She'd know what to do. I could barely get the words out. I couldn't find enough space between my hyperventilated breaths to explain about the voice mail, about Neil being away, about my fears. Were they misplaced? Had I gone crazy?

"Go," she urged. "Leave the house." Just in case.

Neil had our good car at the airport, and I didn't know how far I could make it in the rusty old Volvo station wagon we'd bought when we moved to the country. And where would I go? I grabbed my cell phone, threw on my bulky winter coat and boots, and went to knock on the door of my landlord, who lived in the main house on the same property. Matthew Milburn was a retired physicist. We'd never spoken much, but he seemed trustworthy.

"My father," I said, and began to tell him my story. All my life I'd avoided this very shame, of the knock on a stranger's door asking for help, the admission that my own father had hurt me and might again.

"Is he dangerous?" asked Mr. Milburn. I thought of how my father used to commute to his office in Long Island City with an ax tucked underneath the driver's seat. But that was twenty years ago. In the message he'd sounded eerily calm and determined, like a father who missed his daughter and would do anything to see her.

"Is he dangerous?" Mr. Milburn pressed.

Was he? I hardly knew anymore. To me he was. I knew what it was like to have my back against the stairs, trapped with no place to run. Or to have him pounding on my locked bedroom door. I could still feel his hands on me.

"My counselor said I should show you how much I cared by driving up. I want to see you, talk to you," my father had said in the message.

But why hadn't he asked my permission before coming? And how had he managed to pick the one weekend when Neil was away? Had he planned it this way?

"I think he might be," I told my landlord.

"Don't worry," Mr. Milburn reassured me. He seemed ready for anything. He even had a bomb shelter in his basement.

We'd spend the remainder of the afternoon at home, Mr. Milburn decided, and then head down the road to his girlfriend Gwen's place for dinner. He handed me a throw blanket, pointed me toward a worn leather sofa, and left me alone, staying close by in the office across from the den where he'd settled me. My therapist, for whom I'd left a this-might-be-an-emergency message, had me call her in New York once an hour to check in. She told me to wait there for Neil and then find someplace else to sleep for the night. I sat with the cell phone on my lap, willing Neil to come home.

At ten minutes before six, Mr. Milburn collected me and

put me in his car, and we drove down to his girlfriend's place, past the dairy farm I walked to on my morning constitutionals. "You'll like Gwen," he said, as if we were on our way to a dinner party.

Gwen was ten years younger than Mr. Milburn, silvery-gray-haired and well mannered and kind, cultured and Connecticut-y, while I was a sobbing, snotty Jewish mess in sweatpants with tissues stuck up my sleeves. In her dining room I cried into my graciously prepared plate of pasta. She asked about my father. I was shaking at her table, so we couldn't exactly avoid the topic. I didn't know which was worse, admitting to this refined stranger that I'd become a bad daughter, or that I'd come from such awful parents. To my relief, Mr. Milburn soon piled me back into his car and returned me to what now felt like my new safe house on his couch.

Mercifully, Neil pulled up the driveway. I'd fallen in love with a bookish professor, but it hadn't escaped me that Neil was once a cop.

"Thank God you're home," I said, and briefed him in a rush of words.

"I don't want to freak you out," Neil said, "but we should probably stay in a motel tonight."

We drove north, checking in to a sterile room in Bennington, Vermont. Neil tucked me underneath the thin baby blue fuzz of a polyester motel blanket. Without decent cell reception, or maybe to shield me, he made calls from the pay phone in the parking lot while I turned up the television in the room. Neil phoned the local police station in New York and the Vermont police near the motel to alert them and ask about a restraining order. We were told that if my father bothered me again, he could be arrested for harassment.

What about my mother? I wanted to make sure my father wasn't going to take my refusal out on her when he got home. I asked Neil to call her and make sure she was safe. That call Neil made from our room. I wouldn't get on the phone, but I could hear my mother on the other end. "Safe?" I heard her say. She wanted to kill herself. My father wasn't the problem, I was. How could I not talk to her? Not talk to my brothers? My mother said she was beside herself. *I* was the one hurting her, not him.

*   *   *

After that day I decided to change my life. Each morning I forced myself to meditate or bundle up and take a cold country walk. On my yoga mat, during long drives, in kitchen conversations with Neil, late at night when I couldn't sleep, while reading Eastern philosophy or writing in my journal, I contemplated the meaning of forgiveness. The real kind that has to do with acceptance and moving forward, not the bullshit forgive-and-forget package of lies I'd been trying to swallow for years.

A nearby junk shop had a big sign: *Be good, feel good, do good*. I adopted the saying as my new motto and created a plan for getting my life together. I'd go after my dreams, I swore. I'd live a life my family hadn't imagined possible for me. It wasn't easy or simple, and some days I couldn't stand myself and wanted to die, but each day I forced myself to try. I sat down at my desk and began working harder on my writing. A few months later I had my first short piece published. It was a slight accomplishment, a book review in a yoga magazine, and I was paid fifty bucks, if that, but seeing my byline on glossy paper thrilled and encouraged me. Through those long winter months, I started taking care of my body with solitary sun salutations and sessions on the elliptical at the college gym. By spring, the daily routine of writing and teaching and getting enough exercise and sleep had started to heal me. And I'd pretty much quit drinking. My skin glowed, and I was forty pounds lighter from months of healthy eating. Best of all, I woke up in the mornings feeling hopeful. Somehow I'd made it through the dark tunnel of depression. Maybe what I'd needed all these years was to just leave. My biggest regret was not having made the break sooner.

* * *

Franny called. It had been a long time since I'd heard from her. We'd lost touch while I was in Madison. She never answered her phone and wouldn't call me back when I left messages. So it felt like a miracle when, two or three years later, the phone rang on a mild late-April evening. Franny sounded good, clearheaded. I was elated that she'd found me.

"I only drink once or twice a week now," she said. "And only two drinks, nothing more. I've even gone to a couple of meetings with a friend."

"Wow, that's great," I answered, not knowing what to say. It *was* great.

We talked for a couple of hours. Neil cooked and brought me dinner to eat outside on the lawn where I'd taken the phone. Franny was in Los Angeles. Temporarily, she said, staying with her father.

I was getting married at the end of May, I told her. A small garden wedding on the lawn of the place we rented in the country, a few days after my thirtieth birthday. Would she come?

She had no money for a plane ticket, she said, but wanted very much to be there.

I hesitated before asking Neil while we watched television in bed. Would he fly her in?

He would. He knew how important Franny was to me.

Six weeks later I drove to the train station in Hudson to pick her up. I rolled down the station wagon windows and felt the warm air on my bare arms for the first time since before winter. Everything felt possible again.

Franny came off the train, and we hugged one another hard for a minute or two before widening ourselves out again. Holding hands, arms in a circle, assessing each other. She looked me over. I had fallen in love, been to therapy. I had highlights in my hair and a tiny diamond ring in my nose placed in the long-ago Kathmandu hole, and another on my finger. She was thin, too, but not from sun salutations and country walks, like me. More like a sick person who'd been through cancer treatment and was emerging on the other side, shaky, but with a greater awareness of being alive. She smelled different. Musty. I was shy with her, nervous to ask too many questions about how her last years had been. I worried.

She was still Franny, though. Familiar. Ethereal. I loved her without question. We went back to the house and Franny wrote out place cards, calligraphy-style, in black marker. She was our witness the next morning in town when we signed the wedding papers. I had on white jeans and a white T-shirt and a thick wool cardigan, and Franny took our photograph in front of the town hall. That afternoon we bought our wedding flowers by the bucket from a farm across the road, and Franny arranged them into bouquets and vases.

Our wedding weekend was simple and lovely, magical, even, at least for me, filled with wildflowers and friends who'd come up from the city, driven in from Boston, or flown in from Wisconsin and California to stay with us, or at a shabby inn down the road, or to camp at a nearby campground. But it was unusual in one obvious way. We didn't have parents or siblings surrounding us under the Indian tapestry we used as a make-your-own chuppah. The closest Neil had were his aunt and uncle and two cousins; the closest I had were Franny and Kathy and the rest of my friends.

Though a lingering part of me longed for parents to walk me down the aisle, I felt my family's absence mostly as a relief. Another, hidden part of me half wished I'd had a proper wedding, the kind my mother would have wanted and planned for me. I shooed those thoughts away.

At the ceremony I wore a white tea-length Morgane Le Fay dress with short puff sleeves, my one extravagance. Neil was in a seersucker suit, his hair a mess of curls. Franny, in a borrowed black dress from the sixties, read a poem suggested by her father, "A Sweet Flying Dream" by Lawrence Ferlinghetti.

Afterward, Neil and I sat at a table set for two under the white reception tent, kissing as our few dozen guests clinked utensils to wineglasses. We had a vegetarian buffet and a vegan chocolate cake with a bear bride and groom on top. We danced to Sade and Krishna Das. Neil understood me, and I could be myself with him. Waking me in the early morning from a father nightmare, he would urge me to focus on the good in our lives, on the grass beneath my feet and the leaves on the trees. "Here," he would say, taking me into the woods. "This is what's real."

At the end of the weekend, I was saddest to see Franny go. She was headed to the city. Her mother was living in London by then. I put a bunch of rolled-up twenties in her palm, like my parents used to do for me.

After the wedding, Neil and I moved to Los Angeles so he could take a job at the University of Southern California. For our honeymoon, we took turns driving cross-country through plains and mountains, stopping in national parks and cowboy towns with actual tumbleweed, this time heading all the way west, watching the big sky weave through sunrise, high noon, sunset, and starry night.

SEVENTEEN

WE RENTED A place in a hippie canyon neighborhood off the Pacific Coast Highway. The apartment was an open and ramshackle studio with two tiny closet-like spaces that we used as his-and-hers offices, a loft bed, and a small kitchen set on a platform. Outside was a bathtub with a view of the mountains. From our door you could hike right up into the dry light green hills, walking by yards with horses and skirting snakes on the path, and I did most afternoons before dinner. Our landlord was a Jewish Hare Krishna who lived upstairs, and we had to sneak when we wanted to cook fish. I was making next to nothing, teaching yoga and trying to write. Neil was working on his first book and teaching at USC.

What I wanted more than anything was for us to have a family of our own. A baby, I dreamed. *A baby, a baby, a baby*. This, my new mantra, was all I could think about. I was only thirty-one and my period was regular, so I never imagined I'd have any trouble, but a friend who had children suggested we start trying anyway. And so I dutifully tracked my ovulation and timed the sex we had, reaching my legs to the ceiling afterward. It took me six months of trying.

When the pee stick said positive, I was elated. But I was frightened, too. Could I be a good enough mother? At an office in Beverly Hills for my first prenatal appointment, I sat in flip-flops, waiting for my turn.

Only there was no heartbeat. The doctor came in to explain about miscarriage. Eight weeks pregnant, or not pregnant, with an empty placental sac in my womb, I registered the comfort of the nurse's arm as she drew my blood, and felt hollowed out by the after-hours D&C. *My baby.* I was beyond consolation.

That spring, several months later, I wrote to my mother. It had been almost four years. Experiencing motherhood, however briefly, had made me want my mother. And what did I owe her? I wondered. Over email, I reached out to her about the idea of a relationship in which we might maintain some sort of distant occasional contact. I wrote that I knew she was sorry and that I worried about her. But I was still angry. She wrote back and said she'd seen a counselor who helped her become "more assertive and attuned to my own needs." She said she had failed me, it was true, but she had also loved and nurtured me. She said her therapist had helped her learn that "I was in some ways too good for this world for I didn't see how most humans most often act out of self-interest." *What?* She wanted to build a new relationship, she wrote, but it would have to be about healing and new beginnings. She couldn't let me or my anger destroy her.

I understood, sort of, but didn't write back. It felt completely and utterly impossible. I was her daughter. I was supposed to take responsibility for her now that she was getting older. Only the part of me that should have cared about her no longer existed; this had died, too. I didn't want her anymore. My anger was all that was left. I had nothing else for her.

But it turned out my mother had something she wanted to offer me. A year or two later, Neil received an email from her. My parents were retiring and selling their house. They'd spend winters in Florida and the warmer months in an apartment in Queens. But first they were cleaning out the Rockville Centre house, including my old bedroom. Did I want what was left of my things?

I had left my parents' house that August Sunday years before, not realizing I would never once be back. Before the estrangement, I'd been living in a series of cramped and temporary spaces and hadn't moved my childhood memorabilia along with me. I thought I'd given those things up the day I left. Sentimental as I was, I had mourned the last remains and artifacts of my childhood, but it had never occurred to me to simply ask my parents for them.

Two large boxes arrived in Neil's office. Along with drama club playbills and posters and yearbooks dating from middle school to Vassar, here were my albums of photographs and the odd scrapbook memento from high school and college and Nepal and Israel. My drama class notebooks were there, too. As were my early attempts at writing, including my first short story. In another notebook were drafts of poems I'd written in high school. A blue three-ringed binder was filled with my college poetry.

Mostly there were stacks of cards and letters from high school and college friends, including love letters from my college boyfriend Alex, and a few ambiguous notes from Ben that I once analyzed to death, along with the blue airmail letters my parents had written me when I was in Nepal and Israel, and from before that, even, during my high school summers away. Then I found my diaries. I'd kept a journal on and off since the eighth grade. The entries were sporadic and skipped some years entirely. In them I'd written about my father and the abuse, and I'd struggled with my complicated feelings for him. I'd also kept datebooks faithfully chronicling the activities of my day-to-day life from ninth grade on. The contents of the boxes added up to a surprisingly comprehensive archive. My parents, whether they realized it or not, had sent me the evidence I needed to understand my childhood and my decision.

*   *   *

I couldn't get pregnant again. Not that year and not the next, either. I resisted fertility treatments and instead tried acupuncture and fertility yoga and tinkering with my already healthy diet. By then we'd moved to Cambridge, Massachusetts, where Neil had been offered an assistant professor job at Harvard. I was editing an anthology I'd sold to a publisher in New York about miscarriage; writing for yoga magazines; and teaching a creative writing class at Harvard's version of night school. We lived in a sunny apartment near Inman Square and adopted a dog, Salem, an eccentric and lovable beagle pointer we took to the Harvard Yard dog park before dinner. But all I thought about were babies. The one I'd lost and the one who wouldn't come. We broke down and went to Brigham and Women's Hospital to find out what was wrong. The doctors didn't know. They gave me the fertility drug Clomid. All it did was fill me with an unaccustomed rage. Next up was IUI—intrauterine insemination. Neil walked his still-warm specimen cup of sperm to the hospital room where I lay in stirrups. When that didn't work, we said we would adopt instead. We met with social workers, filled out applications, wrote essays, had our home study, sent the checks, and began the long wait for a toddler from an orphanage in India. Adoption made more sense to me than IVF; the process struck me as beautiful. Why make a new baby when already existing children needed homes? Why did I, of all people, need to share blood or DNA with my child? I suppose, too, I was scared that a biological child of mine would turn out like my father.

And then, after a year and a half on the waiting list and an excruciating, heartbreaking struggle over whether or not to accept a referral for a perhaps profoundly developmentally delayed child we didn't feel ourselves up to taking on, I changed my mind. I decided we *had* to try. By this time I was thirty-five and had been consumed by infertility for four years. I longed more desperately than ever to be pregnant, to breast-feed, to wrap a newborn in a cotton sling and carry her on my chest. I wanted to experience a mother-child relationship not marked by pain and loss. A clinic in Denver, one of the best in the country, would take our insurance. Neil and I went for workups and met the head doctor and the assigned fertility nurse who would guide us through the process. After the initial trip to Denver, I flew to Tucson, Arizona, for a writing residency, soaking up weeks of quiet mornings sitting at the desk in my cottage, working, and late afternoons hiking in the mountains or taking a yoga class before eating a vegetable burrito for dinner. When I returned to Cambridge, I began the shots and drugs and then Neil and I flew back to Colorado for a cycle of IVF.

EIGHTEEN

I REMEMBER BREATHING through labor surges as we drove past the Statue of Liberty on the Brooklyn-Queens Expressway. The car service driver took the Brooklyn Bridge to FDR Drive, and the city was all lit up for Christmas. We were living in Brooklyn during Neil's research sabbatical. Days past my due date and worried about having to be induced, I'd seen an acupuncturist to help start my labor, but nevertheless I was surprised by my water breaking and the mucus plug on the bathroom floor and the reality of even these early contractions. At the hospital, I moaned and breathed and changed positions and tried to let the contractions move through me, but I was bothered by the unwanted antibiotics and the IV drip in my arm and the iPod we forgot to charge and the shower that ran only lukewarm water. My scheduled midwife was away for the holidays, and I was completely overwhelmed by the ferociousness of the pain and wishing I could take it all back or have the baby at home in my bathtub. Neil wore a worried expression. My doula, Tara, massaged my lower back with oils and had Neil rub my shoulders. Because of my decision,

I had no mother to hold my hand and no family huddled up in the waiting room to welcome our baby.

As early morning approached, I'd hardly made any progress with my dilation, despite laboring through killer contractions. My body refused to open up. Wanting to keep things natural, I wouldn't consider Pitocin to urge along my labor or accept the epidural that might have helped me relax. My labor officially stalled. I cried and threw up and cried some more. Eventually I ran a fever.

Neil and Tara fortified themselves with muffins and tall cups of coffee. The nurse came in and checked me for the umpteenth time, charting my nonprogress on the log. Another hour had gone by with nothing to show for it. Neil sat in a blue hospital chair in the corner of the room and took his glasses off, rubbing his eyes and temples, willing himself to stay awake. Tara set her coffee down on the window ledge and gave a tentative suggestion: "Is there anything you need to let go of? Is there any reason you might be afraid to release, to let the baby come, to become a mother?"

And then I was done. Done trying to hold on, done trying to be perfect. After that it was yes to the drugs, and hours later when the doctor said I needed it, yes to an emergency C-section. That night on the surgery table I shivered with fever. Neil held my hand and talked me through.

My baby was here! My baby. *I didn't know he'd be so beautiful,* I said when the doctor showed him to me before hurrying him off to the NICU for observation. (A necessary precaution, she said, because of my long labor and fever.)

Neil wasn't allowed to stay in my room and went home

to Brooklyn for a few hours to sleep. Before dawn, after hours of my nonstop asking, the night nurse decided I was recovered enough from surgery to see my son. She pushed my wheelchair to the NICU and arranged me in a chair. Finally he was brought to me. He smelled like sunshine. I held him to my chest and offered him my breast. We rocked and nursed and I sang to him and knew I would never let go.

I hadn't been certain I would know how to mother. Yet somehow I knew just the way to hold him, how to nourish, how to caress, how to sing to him, how to rock and comfort. "Edelweiss" was our first lullaby, and there would be many more. Neil arrived back at the hospital, and as morning broke, we were together. We were a family.

*   *   *

We named him Lucien, *light*.

After six weeks I could take the baby and the dog and make a slow loop around Prospect Park with the stroller, stopping in the frigid early-February air to undo my nursing bra and slip him beneath my coat or change his diaper on a park bench. I slept with Lucien, fed him, carried him on my chest, talked to him, and found I could usually make things better. When he wouldn't stop crying, at least I could hold him.

Sometimes, when taking care of Lucien, I thought about my mother. Growing up, I'd craved her touch but hadn't known how to ask for it. Where Lucien's skin felt like an extension of mine, my mother's had always felt foreign to me. Hers was, if not a stranger's skin, then a visitor's. I regretted and grieved our lack of comfort with each other. But perhaps she once felt as close to her babies as I did to mine. Maybe I used to look at her the way Lucien looked at me. I started thinking of her with a little less anger and a little more compassion. I allowed myself to miss her.

* * *

Back when we lived in Cambridge and attended Harvard faculty parties with bold-named professors, I tried not to break down when asked the normal questions about family, like where I grew up and where my parents lived. I tried not to be overcome by my guilt and shame. *We're estranged*, I learned to say. *It's complicated*. Once, after giving a reading where I touched on the abuse, a writer came up to me to tell me she was in my mother's position. "I am your mother," she said. Just that week she had gathered up her courage and her child and left her husband.

My New York therapist referred me to a graduate school classmate of hers who had an office on Massachusetts Avenue. Each week I sat on my new psychologist's couch, examining each painful pushed-down memory. The more I talked, the more I remembered. She taught me that my relationship with my parents continued on whether I spoke to them or not. She gave me wise counsel, and when I needed her to, she mothered me. Eventually, after over a decade of on-again, off-again sessions, I came to understand that I'd done nothing wrong. I began shedding the guilt and shame like a dead skin. The estrangement was my way of saving myself. When I made the decision to walk away from my parents, I made the decision to be happy.

*   *   *

Not long after Lucien was born, Neil received an offer with more money and tenure from the University of British Columbia, and on something of a sleep-deprived whim, we decided to move coasts and countries with our six-month-old baby. By the time Lucien turned one, we'd bought an old fixer-upper with a porch out front, a basement rental apartment to help us with the mortgage, and room for a vegetable garden in the backyard. I planted more kale and lettuce and tomatoes than we could eat. I grew peas and garlic and tall rows of corn. We painted Lucien's bedroom gentle shades of green and yellow, and soon IKEA bins filled with wooden toys and used books and stuffed animals lined the floors. I took him to music and dance and drama and swim class at the community center. We became regulars at the playground a few blocks away with the soaring pine trees. As I pushed him on the swings under them, we sang together, "This Little Light of Mine," "Itsy-Bitsy Spider," "The Wheels on the Bus." We visited the neighborhood libraries so often the librarians knew Lucien by name. We made friends with other young parents on our block, people we could call when we needed help with child or dog or garden, people who could ask the same of us. We shopped at a farmers' market by a small lake and went for walks in a forest in the middle of the city where our dog, Salem, could run off-leash and Lucien could pretend we were in the Hundred Acre Wood. For several years I wrote a twice-weekly motherhood blog for a magazine, earning my first steady writing paycheck, and taught a class in the creative writing department at the university. Mostly I took care of Lucien. The more I mothered my child, the more my yearning for a mother of my own dimmed. It never disappeared, not completely. Still the desire resurfaced, taking me by surprise, at the big moments, for him and for me.

Here are the times when you wish you had a mother: When you can't get pregnant and when you finally do; when you have your baby and are holding him for the first time. When you buy your first house and try to fix it up; at your first bookstore reading; when your husband's research makes it into the newspapers; when he's having a mass removed and you wait alone in the hospital of a brand-new city to hear that it's not cancer; when your son has his first birthday and his fifth; on his first day of kindergarten. When the writing disappointments come; when marriage gets hard; when you and your toddler have the flu and your husband is in Finland or Sweden or Hong Kong. When friendships end. When you need someone to show you how.

A mother, yes—what I wouldn't do for one. But not mine. Despite my ambivalence about her, I was certain Lucien and Neil and I were better off on our own.

*   *   *

I was sitting in a café in Vancouver, writing, when my sister-in-law Rachel emailed and asked if she could phone me. We hadn't spoken in seven years. Josh didn't know she was calling, Rachel said, but she and my other sister-in-law, Tamara, were uncomfortable with the sometimes harsh and weirdly authoritarian way my parents acted around their children. They were worried about leaving the grandchildren alone with them, despite the assurances of my brothers. And Rachel and Tamara had a question for me. Had it been sexual? Or just physical?

Just physical, I answered, briefly describing the violence and the name-calling we'd grown up with. She already knew about the arguments and manipulations. And then we hung up.

I can't know what my sister-in-law did with that information. But sitting in the café while my babysitter clock ticked, I was disgusted with myself for parroting her words—*just physical*. For minimizing the damage he'd done, as if somehow it was okay for children to be exposed to the threat of physical abuse as long as it wasn't sexual. And yet I understood how impossible it must have felt to go up against my parents, even for a tough New York City lawyer. Maybe she did decide that *just physical* counted. Maybe she'd made certain to keep her children close. I hoped so.

*   *   *

We were on the back steps the first time Lucien asked me. He was eating raspberries I'd picked off the vines that ran along the fence separating our garden from the neighbor's yard. His face was pink and sweet with the evidence of them. He was very young, very verbal. Perhaps two and a half? Stained fingers. Light brown curly hair left to grow wild. We'd been playing with the garden hose. He looked up at me.

"Mommy, do you have a mommy?"

My breath caught.

"Yes, baby," I said. "I do."

* * *

A year passed. Two. Although Neil and I were already overwhelmed by the relentlessness of parenting a young child and the tricky finances of life as a college professor and a freelance writer in an incredibly expensive city, I convinced him that we should go back to Denver, where we had a frozen embryo from our first IVF cycle. Neil was ambivalent. "I loved being an only child," he told me. "We can't afford it," he said, any of it. Not the procedure (which our Canadian health insurance wouldn't cover) and not raising a second child. We couldn't even afford to fix our roof, and the walls of our bedroom were mildewed with drips from the never-ending Vancouver rain. But I persisted. We could use the last of Neil's parents' house money. I could try to pick up more freelance assignments, and Neil could take on an extra summer school class.

For a couple of years after having Lucien, I'd been un-sure about trying again, too. Our baby was a bright, super-sweet, soulful, silly, and creative nonstop joy machine. Wasn't that enough? Plus, Neil had his *work,* and now I had mine. With one child, Lucien had all my love and attention, and I could manage a sort of career without family help or a full-time nanny. We could even occasionally afford for Lucien and me to tag along on a research trip with Neil. We went to New York and took Lucien to the Museum of Natural History; we traveled with Lucien to Paris and stayed for a month. "See!" Neil said, though Lucien and I didn't make it out of our arrondissement more than a half-dozen times. But we sipped hot chocolate at the top of the Pompidou on his third birthday, and shared a magical taxi ride home from a dinner party near the Eiffel Tower. One afternoon a dad in the metro gave Lucien his daughter's balloon just because. At home in Vancouver, I wrote during the still of naptime. A friend from yoga class brought her girls over, and we went for a walk in the cemetery across the street. She said I was smart, that my life seemed sane; she envied me.

But I tortured myself about what it would mean for Lucien to be an only child. Once, a neighbor friend men-tioned a saying she'd heard that one kid was practice, two a family. The comment rattled around in my brain no matter how many times Neil or Kathy (mother to three children) tried to convince me of its stupidity.

Oh, how I wanted that second baby, sane or not. In time, Neil did, too.

One last try, we said. We would do everything right. We took great care with every hormone patch and injection. We even ate the same veggie burgers at the same vegetarian restaurant in Denver. We allowed ourselves to be hopeful and think it would work.

When it didn't, when things went terribly wrong, a horrible night at an emergency room in Vancouver, and then a few days later a negative pregnancy blood test, I just wanted to go home.

NINETEEN

WE RETURNED TO Brooklyn after almost five years in Canada. Neil was on sabbatical, a leave he'd extended with the help of a visiting-professor position at Princeton. Though I was closer to my past in New York, and to my parents, I felt most at home in this city, the place that first gave me a glimpse of independence when I was a teenager and bought my train ticket away from Rockville Centre and smoked a cigarette on the platform, ascending the Penn Station escalator an hour later.

We rented the second floor of a house in East Williamsburg with a small community garden down the street, across from a Catholic church and school, and another couple of blocks away, a park with a playground and small dog run. The L train stop was right around the corner. Flowers managed to thrive in gated boxes on the sidewalk; garbage gently blew with the breeze, like dandelion seeds.

I began looking back at my childhood with a sense of remove, as if screening a Super 8 movie. Slightly out-of-focus sepia images flashed of birthday parties and car trips and watching my brothers' baseball games from the bleachers, and the bad days, too, the angry voices and raised hands.

That was my life then. I came to accept it, all of it. But accepting it didn't mean I'd see them. The distance enabled me to reinvent myself, learn new ways of living, become the sort of mother I dreamed of being.

*　　*　　*

My parents used to say they wished for me a difficult child; they hoped I'd have a child like me. And Lucien *is* just like me. He's creative and passionate and sensitive and strong-willed. Almost always we're easy together. We start and end the day by snuggling in one of our beds. We read we play we discuss we walk we eat we hug we laugh. Some days, when I get frustrated, when I want him to listen and just do what I say without so many questions, I hear myself growing sharper and less patient. "Why are you being stern?" Lucien asks. As I close my eyes and breathe deep and struggle to regain my equilibrium, I can't help but think about my father, and in those moments I find myself understanding how he let his anger fly. It's easier to yell than to stop and breathe. And while I can't imagine ever laying hands on my child, no matter what, I recognize the frustration and exhaustion and impatience and even anger, the close relatives of rage, that sometimes stir within me.

*　　*　　*

On an early-winter day twenty years after college graduation, I boarded the train from Grand Central to Poughkeepsie, listening to Billy Joel's *Summer, Highland Falls* on repeat, and checked in at the Vassar Alumnae House. Walking around campus, I noticed, mostly, how incredibly close to one another all the buildings were. We only had to roll out of bed to be fed and educated and entertained. It was all there, handed to us. How very young we were, how beautifully innocent. (Never mind how we imagined ourselves worldly and jaded.) How privileged. Despite their problems, my parents had offered me a better life than they had.

Franny and I had a terrible, irreversible argument one Christmas in London several weeks after my miscarriage, when I needed her and felt she wasn't there for me. Wrong or right, *that's* the break I regret, the one it seems there's no turning back from. All these years later and I've never run into her on a city street, never had the chance to place my son in her arms. To this day, I dream about her. I picture the two of us together, back at school and young again. We're on a walk to the Vassar farm, studying at the library, or laughing in our dorm room. How fortunate I was to have those years with Franny. I ask about her when I stumble across a mutual acquaintance. Every year or two, I allow myself to check her Facebook page for clues to her life, though I don't dare send a friend request. For a while she lived in the Yucatán and worked at an animal shelter, saving street dogs. She made art. Nowadays Franny and her artist husband live in upstate New York with their son. He's just a couple of years younger than Lucien. How I long to pick up the phone, to send a letter, to show up on her doorstep. (Oh, to have our boys meet and play.) But I know I won't.

I've decided not to intrude, to let Franny go as my parents have let me go, to say a final and lasting goodbye. I know I'll never have a friend like that again.

*　　*　　*

I've been back to Rockville Centre a couple of times, my heart pounding and my nerves firing like mad the whole way, even though my parents have long since moved. A few years ago, I went to a high school reunion, and once Neil and Lucien and I visited my childhood friend Karen and her husband and children when they were staying with Karen's parents. Lots of my classmates live in or near town, but not my friends. We were the drama kids and the freaks and the nerds and assorted outcasts and rebels who wanted to get away and did.

Sometimes I bring Lucien to the Metropolitan Museum of Art, and afterward we go to Bloomingdale's for frozen yogurt. This, the same Manhattan store where my mother used to take me shopping on special occasions. The lingerie department where she bought her bras and underwear sits on the same floor as the café. When I was pregnant, I went there all the time for the chocolate frozen yogurt, and maybe for something more.

*　　*　　*

We were at our kitchen table in Brooklyn, eating oatmeal with honey and banana slices.

"Mommy, do you have a mommy?" Lucien, then five, got up the nerve to ask me again. "Where is your mommy? Who is your mommy's mommy?"

I answered the best I could. Honestly, breezily. Maybe that alone was a lie. "My grandmother's name was Kay. She died years ago. My mother lives part-time in Queens and part-time in Florida."

Lucien said he wanted to meet them.

"Not all mommies and daddies are nice, babe," I explained, an oversimplification that I hoped would satisfy him. "Most are, almost always. But sometimes, unfortunately, there are mean mommies and mean daddies. Like in *Cinderella*. Or *Hansel and Gretel*. That's the kind I had. But now I have you and Daddy."

The questions faded. Life resumed: the morning rush on the subway to school, afternoon pickups and playgrounds, library visits and trampoline class and chorus, bath time and stories and bedtime, Sundays in Prospect Park, a few summertime weeks in the country. I made plans with old and new friends and arranged playdates for Lucien and sat on park benches talking to the other moms and dads after school. I lingered when Neil and I hugged in the kitchen. I wanted Lucien to understand that we were a part of something and that we were loved.

Each year the questions returned with more sophistication, and I dared to tell him more of the truth, to allow him to see some of my sadness. He'd soak in the bathtub while Neil cooked, Lucien playing with pirate ships and swooshing around a striped washcloth and asking me question after question about my parents. I sat on the bath mat next to my beautiful boy, dispensing soap and fielding his inquiries, hoping to strike the right balance between tenderness and truth.

One thing. He knows how wrong it is to hit or call someone bad names. Another: He knows I have rules—wash your hands when you get home, clean your room, put your dishes in the sink, no video games, in bed reading long before lights out—but that I try not to ever yell. Lucien knows, of course, that no matter what, I would never leave him.

* * *

Sometimes I let myself think about what the estrangement must be like for my parents. For my mother, who has missed so much of her daughter's life and has never met her grandchild. For my father, who, despite the good he did for me, has to be reminded daily of his long-ago mistakes. How horrific and unfair my decision must seem to them. How miserly and capricious and mean they must find me.

And yet. After all these years, I feel settled with my decision to remain estranged from my parents. I don't crave a last-minute reunion, nor will I attempt a last-ditch effort at reconciliation before they die. The peace I make with my parents and brothers is a quiet, interior, personal one. Remembering my mother's fingernails scratching my back, my father saying how proud he was of me. How my brothers protected me in their room during the fighting. How they once drove all the way from college in St. Louis to see me in a school play. The books my mother read to me under her sunflower-gold comforter, the drives my father took me on. The way he'd caress my cheek with the back of his hand. When Lucien is older, I'll tell him about those times, too.

*   *   *

When Lucien was seven, we moved one last time, to Maine. We traded in our cozy but cramped rental apartment in Brooklyn and bought an infinitely more affordable nineteenth-century farmhouse in town. A house with a barn and a shaded porch and a wooden swing tied to a pine tree in a picture-postcard backyard, close to the liberal arts college where Neil would chair the sociology department. I would have a room of my own to write in, and Lucien would get to grow up a nature boy. Until our move-in day, we'd stay at a small summer cottage we'd rented in the woods, a ten-minute walk through the forest to a private dock on the lake.

When we arrived at the cabin after stopping to see friends along the way that weekend in Connecticut and Boston, it was hot and late. Neil said he'd get dinner started. Lucien and I put on bathing suits and bug spray and ran down to the water with Salem right behind us. The lake was cool and too beautiful and calm not to jump in. Lucien stripped down and skinny-dipped by the dock. Salem made her runs between forest woods and dusky water and back. Lucien and I swam together, laughing, submerged to our shoulders.

Soon it would be bedtime, and we had dinner to eat and teeth to brush and faces to wash and books to read, but we stayed in the water as the sun went down. We floated on our blue dollar-store noodles arranged like personal boats supporting our arms and knees and backs, feeling safe and happy and free.

AUTHOR'S NOTE

In writing this memoir, I drew from old journals and notebooks and letters, and from more recent correspondence and interviews with people from my childhood. Mostly, though, I drew on my memory. While understanding that memory is subjective, elusive, and deeply personal, I have remained true to my recollection of events and conversations. Some names, including names of family members, have been changed.

ACKNOWLEDGMENTS

Adam Eaglin is incomparably thoughtful and dedicated, hardworking and kind. Every day I feel lucky that I get to work with him. Adam, you knew just the book I should write and how to make it happen. Thank you to Elyse Cheney for embracing this project. Thanks also to Alex Jacobs for all his input, and to Alice Whitwham and Leah Fry.

I am forever indebted to my editor Shannon Welch for her taste, honesty, vision, and care. Knowing I could trust your stellar judgment made it possible for me to write this book. Thank you to John Glynn for his guidance, especially during the final months. I'm also grateful for the exceptional work of so many at Scribner, including (the fantastic) Kate Lloyd, Ashley Gilliam, Taylor Noel, Laura Wise, and Jaya Miceli, and for the support of Roz Lippel and Nan Graham.

David Blum gave me a chance and a bighearted first home for my story. Taylor Antrim suggested I write about being estranged from my parents. As did Rebecca Walker years before. Jen Marshall, Emily Bazelon, and Dani Shapiro generously offered assistance. Special thanks to Danielle Friedman for seeing something in those early pages, for telling me to keep going, and for a decade of 24/7 good advice. Danielle, Daphne Kalotay, Karen Levin, Cassandra Neyenesch, and Leah Vincent read chapters or full drafts and gave important feedback. Thank you to Melanie Weiss and Rabbi Rachel Isaacs.

Many people from my childhood shared their memories over email and phone, on Facebook and in person, and fact-checked mine. Ann Klotz and Seth Orbach were wonderful. Particular thanks to my Rockville Centre classmates who enthusiastically responded to questions big and small: Julie Hansen for remembering the fear, Jason Maniscalco for all things drama, Michael Ezra for all things Hebrew school, and to Allison Fishman Task and the "scholars" and drama club kids for remembering the details. And to Stefanie Zelkind and Monica Fields for letting me. In addition to reading, Karen Levin thoughtfully answered my (sometimes daily) questions. Katherine Brennan contributed invaluable insights about my family. I treasure our long and sustaining friendship.

Over the course of writing, I was also buoyed by Cassandra Neyenesch (again!) and Emily Barman, both of whom provided regular doses of friendship, beauty, and encouragement.

Thanks to Lucien's teachers in New York and Maine, whose commitment and affection meant that I didn't have to worry while I worked. To Rebecca Dickson in Vancouver for those precious writing hours.

The Virginia Center for the Creative Arts, the Omega Women's Leadership Center, and the Catwalk Institute provided quiet settings away from family obligations.

Acknowledgments

Isaac Axtell and Lucy Sullivan kept me healthy, as did the teachings of B. K. S. Iyengar, and his student (and my friend) Marla Apt, as well as the Iyengar Institute in New York.

My conversations with Linda Luz-Alterman about child abuse, family dysfunction, trauma, and estrangement helped me write this book, and much more. Thank you.

My husband Neil Gross will always be my first and best reader. He has read countless pages, offering hundreds (thousands?) of hours of editorial services. All that and nightly dinners! Thank you, most of all, for your unwavering and oh so supportive love, for understanding me better than anyone, for making a family with me, and for always believing in my dreams.

Lucien. You are a night sky filled with stars. You are deepest woods. You are the ocean. You are my companion and my charge and my inspiration and the reason I could finally write this book. ILYMTYLM.